Zany Jewellery

If you're feeling bored on a wet Saturday afternoon, why not make some jewellery from all those leftover bits and pieces lying around the house. Rubber, paper, pasta, ribbons, wool – anything you can find! Make presents for your friends and family for next to nothing!

dedication
For my darling daughter
Jessica Rose Neuritza Moxley

ACKNOWLEDGEMENTS
Many thanks to the following: Fimo for supplying fimo; Hobby Horse for supplying beads; Elinor Mulligan for her help in making arm bands and badges; Spomenka Mircovic for her help in making necklaces.

ZANY
JEWELLERY
Juliet Bawden

Illustrated by Chris Evans
Cartoons by Nick Duffy

A Magnet Book

First published as a paperback original 1989
by Magnet Paperbacks
Michelin House, 81 Fulham Road, London SW3 6RB
Text copyright © 1989 Juliet Bawden
Illustrations copyright © 1989 Chris Evans and Nick Duffy
Printed in Great Britain by Cox and Wyman

ISBN 0 416 13352 5

This paperback is sold subject to the condition
that it shall not, by way of trade or otherwise,
be lent, re-sold, hired out or otherwise circulated
without the publisher's prior consent in any form
of binding or cover other than that in which
it is published and without a similar condition
including this condition being imposed
on the subsequent purchaser.

Contents

INTRODUCTION	6
TOOLS AND MATERIALS	10
Tools	10
Findings	11
Threads and wires	13
Chains and links	14
FIMO	19
Mould-making	21
Animal shapes	22
Christmas jewellery	26
BEADS	31
Beads from paper	32
Beads from clay	34
Baker's clay	38
Decorating beads	39
Bead weaving	42
NECKLACES AND BRACELETS	46
Threading	46
Projects	49
Putting on the Glitz!	53
EARRINGS	61
Hoops	63
Zoo earrings	64
Flower earrings	66
Dangling earrings	67
SEWING JEWELLERY	71
KNITTED AND WOVEN JEWELLERY	75
PAPIER MACHE JEWELLERY	79
RIBBONS	82
Ribbon flowers	84
CHEAP AND CHEERFUL!	86
Food	86
Natural sources	88
Balloons	90
Tights	94
SUPPLIERS	96

Introduction

Making your own jewellery is fun! There are lots of very exciting beads in the shop and many you can buy by mail order. This book shows you how to put them together in interesting ways.

For those of you who are feeling impoverished, there is a cheap and cheerful section at the end of the book which shows you how to make jewellery for next to nothing.

The stars at the top of each page show you how difficult the project is to make. One star means a project is easy; two stars mean that it is a little more difficult; and three stars mean that you may need an adult to help you.

You can find the components for making jewellery in lots of unlikely places. For example, in any large stationers in the form of brightly coloured plastic or metal paperclips which you simply link together. Or they sell miniature bulldog clips, and plastic clothes pegs that are only 3 cm long – these can be attached to a cord or a line to make a fun necklace.

Electrical departments with their arrays of flex and insulated wire are another source of design inspiration. Make necklaces by threading different coloured elastic bands or the tops of balloons onto electric cable. Make beads from cut-up plastic straws (especially the 'bendy' ones), bits of plastic and telephone wire.

Look in department stores for Christmas tree decorations. Thread these together and make flamboyant jewellery for Christmas parties.

And you can even find the materials for jewellery in toy shops. Make a necklace by threading together brightly coloured wooden beads, interspersed with small toys from Christmas crackers or miniature dolls' house toys and models. Thread these onto a piece of plastic, a length of rubber or a leather thong. Make brooches from small plates of dolls' house food with brooch backs glued onto them. Thread dolls' house pots and pans onto a shoelace to make a necklace.

You can buy plastic and rubber creepy crawlies, skeletons, bats, snakes and dinosaurs in toy shops. As the rubber tends to be very thin, they can be pierced easily with a pin and threaded singly or as a gruesome collection onto jump rings and earring clips to make earrings.

With the current interest in beads and accessories and their rise in price, this book shows you how to make your own jewellery at a fraction of what it would cost to buy. Some of the ideas use conventional bought beads and jewellery parts, other ideas can be made for a few pennies. The materials take up very little room, and for the most part can be stored in a shoe box or biscuit tin.

Making jewellery is one way that you can save your pocket money for other things, and who knows, it may even be the start of a career in making and selling jewellery. Have lots of fun!

Tools And Materials
TOOLS

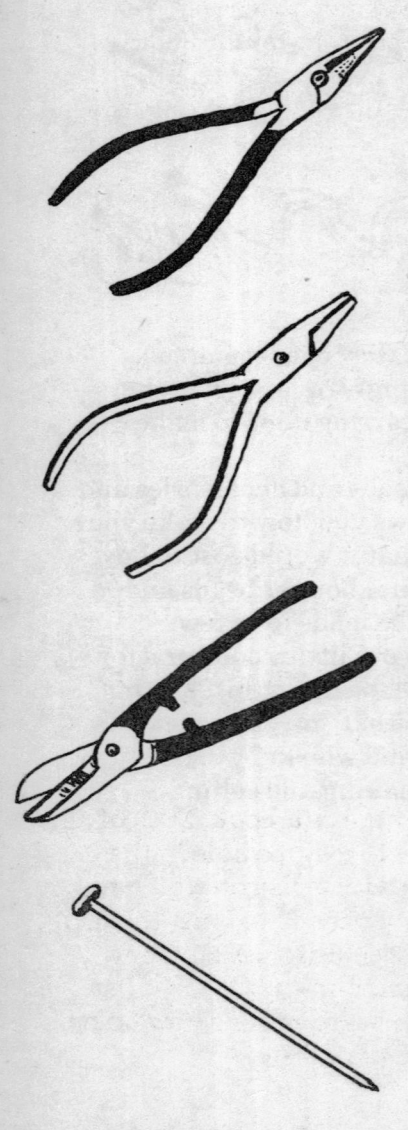

You do not need many tools for jewellery making. The three that are most useful are:

1 A pair of round-nosed jewellers' pliers. These are used for twisting wire into different shapes and for making loops at the end of pins. They are round in section. These are available from **Hobby Horse** (see p96).
2 A pair of flat-nosed jewellers' pliers. These are used to squeeze the ends of wire together, for example when closing a jump ring. They are D-shaped in section. These are available from **Hobby Horse** (see p96).
3 A pair of tin snips for cutting wire. These are available from hardware or DIY shops.

If you are using bugle beads or rocailles (tiny beads) it is useful to have a beading needle. This is a very long fine sewing needle. It is essential to have one of these for bead weaving.

FINDINGS

A 'finding' is the metal mount to which a piece of jewellery is attached. There are many different findings for earrings, brooches, bracelets, necklaces, etc. They come in such a variety of metals and styles that only the ones most commonly used are mentioned below.

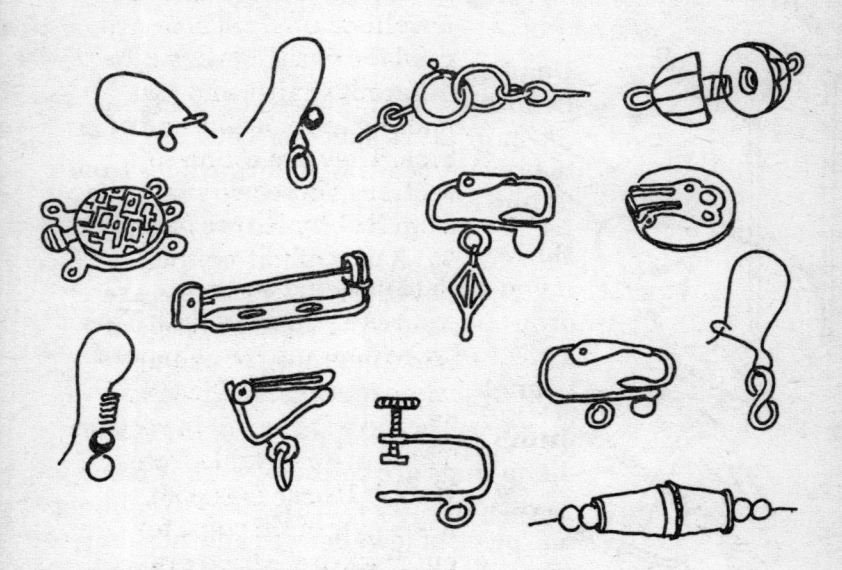

Findings for earrings

For pierced ears you will need a stud or a hook. Both of these are pieces of wire which go through a hole in the ear. Some studs and hooks come with a disc on which to stick beads, others have loops from which to hang them.

Note: for pierced ears it is advisable to use silver or gold-plated findings to prevent infection.

Earring findings for unpierced ears either screw on or clip on. They also have either loops or discs.

Head pins and eye pins

Beads are usually threaded onto head pins or eye pins. These are pre-cut pieces of wire, and come in various lengths.

Head pins look like dressmakers' pins without a pointed end. Beads rest on the head.

Eye pins have a loop or eye at one end for suspending beads.

Bead cup
Bead cups sit on the end of head pins, like miniature saucers. They are used to prevent beads with large holes from falling off.

Bail
If you wish to suspend a cone or drop-shaped bead you use a bail. This is a piece of wire bent into the shape of a triangle.

Jump ring
Jump rings are split rings. They come in various sizes and are used to connect one piece of jewellery to another. For example, you can hang two or three eye pins or head pins from one jump ring, and then hang the jump ring from the earclip or wire.

Spacing bar

A spacing bar is a pretty, decorative piece of metal with a loop at either end. It is used for hanging beads, as an alternative to pins.

THREADS AND WIRES

Copper and silver wire are the most commonly used in jewellery making and they come in many thicknesses. The thickness is commonly known as the SWG (Standard Wire Gauge), or dimensions are given in millimetres. Wires that are 0.4mm and 0.6mm thick are most commonly used in earring making. The 0.6mm wire holds its shape better than the 0.4mm and so is suitable for making jump rings or bails.

When choosing thread consider the following: Is the thread going to show? Is it strong enough for the beads? Is it the correct thickness for the holes in the beads?

Nylon gut is ideal for young people to use as it is easy to thread without a needle.

Tiger tail, a very strong nylon-coated steel thread, is ideal for heavy beads. It too can be used without a needle.

Fine brass wire or **nylon thread** is ideal for fine beads such as rocailles. Again it is not necessary to use a needle.

Waxed terylene is a very strong, all-purpose thread which is easy to use without a needle and comes in various thicknesses.

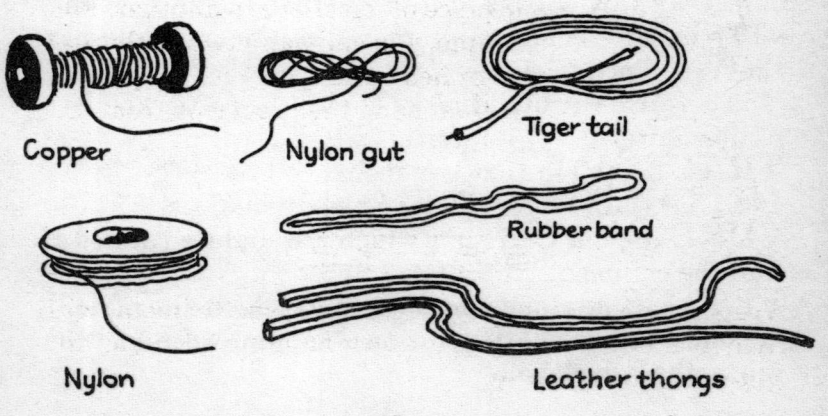

Laces made from rubber are great for fun or junk jewellery and are available from Hobby Horse (see Stockists, p96).

Leather thongs are good for making ethnic jewellery and for beads with large holes.

If you wish to knot between beads for a decorative effect use silk or thick cotton.

CHAINS AND LINKS

When working with beads, it is useful to make links that will join one element to another. Chains consist of links that are joined together.

There are various kinds of chains the better known patterns are:

TRACE Oval links of equal size.
BELCHER large circular links of equal size.
CURB regular oval links which are slightly twisted so that the chain will lie flatter.
FETTER has long and short links which alternate.
Until the Industrial Revolution all chains were made by the method given below.

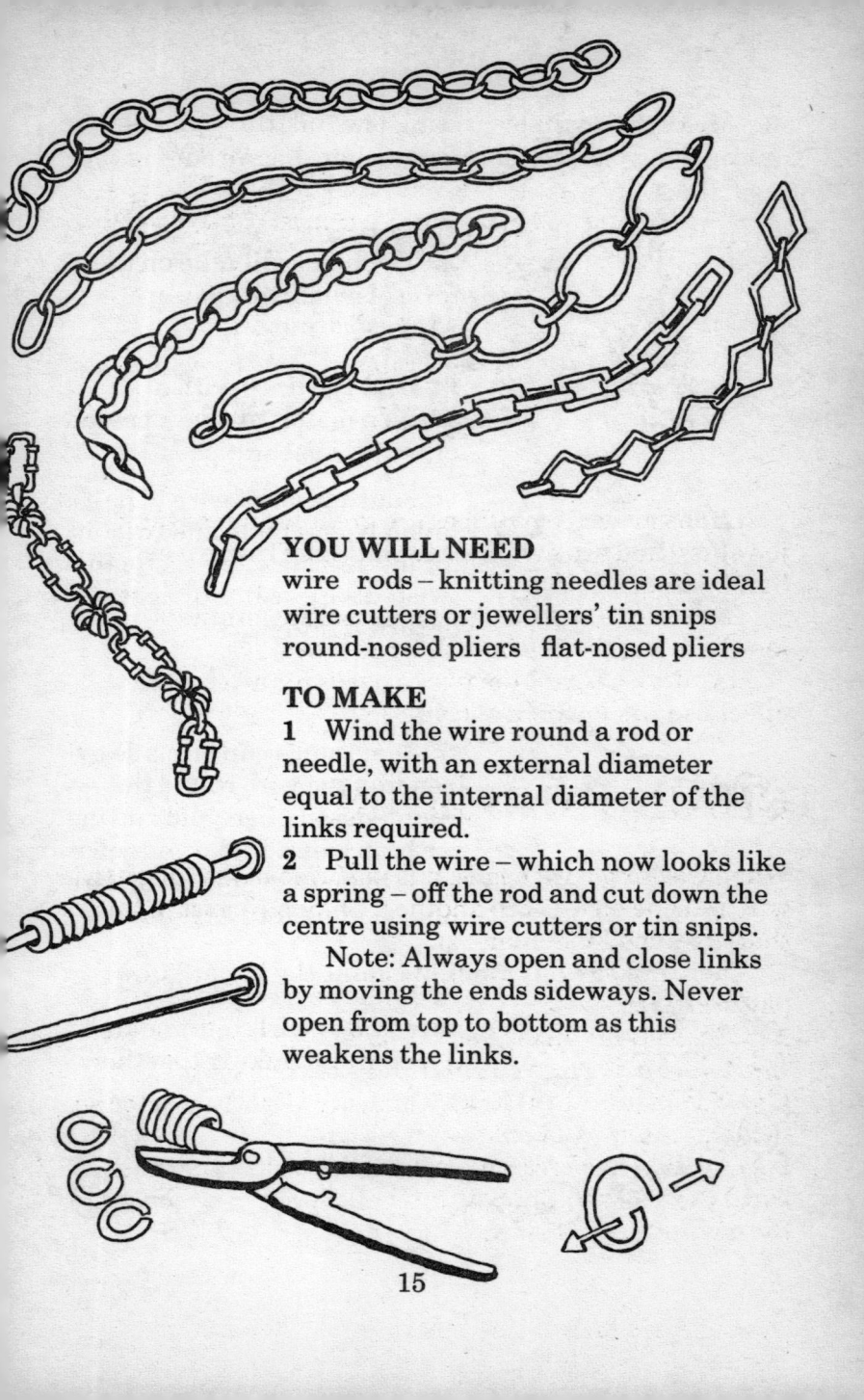

YOU WILL NEED
wire rods – knitting needles are ideal
wire cutters or jewellers' tin snips
round-nosed pliers   flat-nosed pliers

TO MAKE
1 Wind the wire round a rod or needle, with an external diameter equal to the internal diameter of the links required.
2 Pull the wire – which now looks like a spring – off the rod and cut down the centre using wire cutters or tin snips.

Note: Always open and close links by moving the ends sideways. Never open from top to bottom as this weakens the links.

3 Make the chain by passing one link through another and closing between flat-nosed pliers before adding the next links.

IDEAS

✴ The links will take on the form of whatever they are wrapped around.

✴ Beat the links with a wooden mallet to give a beaten or tooled appearance.

✴ Fold a piece of wire in half link it over a hook and twist it for interesting effects. Use the twisted wire as it is or beat it or turn it into links.

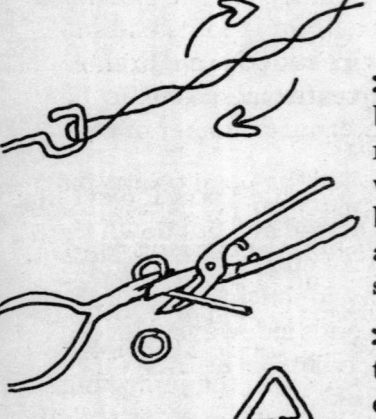

✴ Jump rings can be made by bending the wire round the round-nosed pliers and cutting with tin snips. Make your own bails but cutting pieces of wire and bending into a triangular shape.

✴ Make pearl chains by threading pearls onto small eyepins and linking together.

Findings for necklaces

Many of the findings used for making earrings are also used for making necklaces; for example, jump rings and eye pins can be used in drop necklaces.

Split rings
Split rinks look like miniature key rings and are used with a bolt ring to do up a necklace.

There are various types of screw clasps which may also be used to do up necklaces.

French crimp (crimping bead)
If you are using a thread such as Tiger Tail, you will not be able to tie knots in its end so you will have to use a French crimp or crimping bead.

TO USE
1 Thread the beads onto the 'Tiger Tail' (TT for short).
2 Thread the crimping bead onto the end of the TT.
3 Thread the end of the TT through the loop on the bolt ring or through the jump ring when finishing the other end of the necklace.

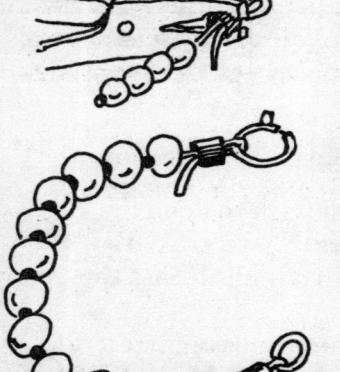

4 Take the end of the TT back through the crimping bead, and pull tight so that the beads are close to the crimping bead.
5 Squeeze the crimping bead tightly with a pair of flat-nosed pliers: this will hold the TT firmly thus stopping it from moving.
6 Cut off any excess TT.

Necklaces may also be finished with hook and eye fastenings.

Box clasp
If you are making a multi-stranded necklace you will need a box clasp fastening.

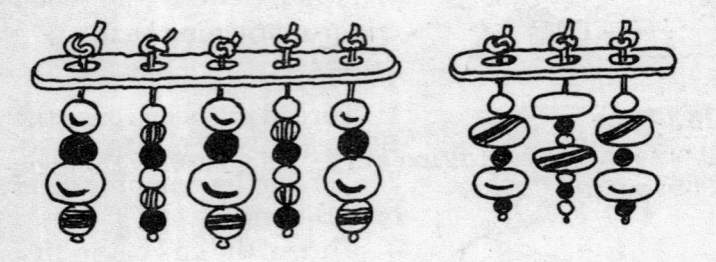

Spacing bars
If you are making a choker or just wish to keep the strands separate, use spacing bars. These are bars with holes at regular intervals through which to pass the thread.

There are of course, many other kinds of fastening. You will soon find out which is most suitable for your purpose.

Fimo

Fimo is a modelling material which comes in a variety of colours and can be moulded, carved, marbled, varnished and baked in an ordinary domestic oven to set. You can also make moulds from it.

TECHNIQUES

Kneading
Before working with fimo it is necessary to knead the fimo to make it soft and pliable. The heat from your hands should do this. Just take a ball of fimo in your hand and squeeze it.

Rolling out
Roll out fimo with a rolling pin in the same way that you roll out pastry.

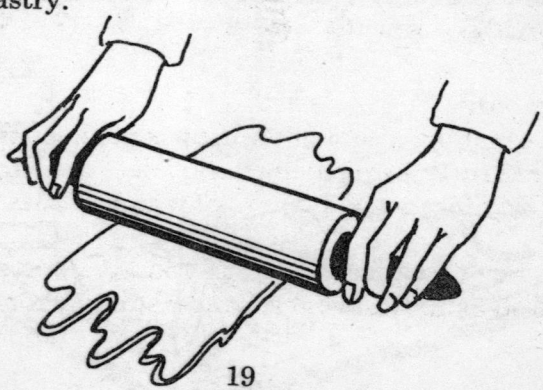

Modelling
Cut and shape bits of fimo to form such items as leaves and flowers.

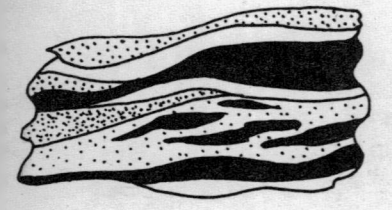

Marbelizing
Mix two or more colours and knead them together to obtain a marbled effect.

Hardening
(An oven is used here. Be cautious and make sure an adult is around and that you have permission to use the oven.) To harden, pre-heat an oven to 140 C (275 F, Gas Mark 1). Cover a baking tray with aluminium foil and put the object to be baked onto the foil. Bake for 15 to 20 minutes depending on the size of the object. It will still be pliable, but check that the object doesn't overcook or else it will go brown.

Varnishing

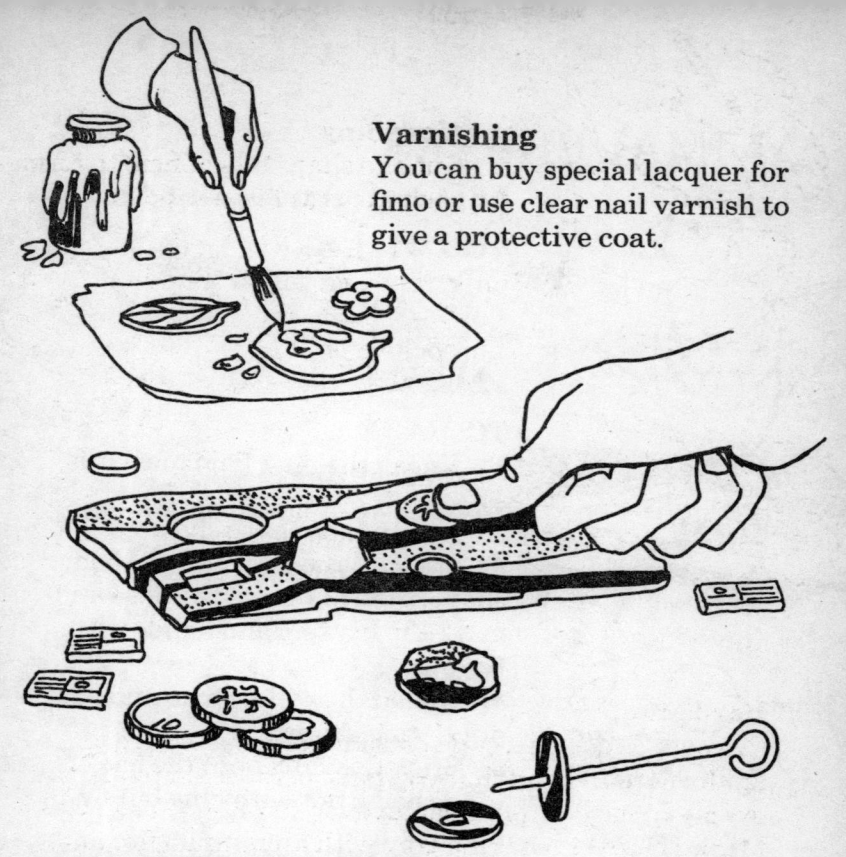

You can buy special lacquer for fimo or use clear nail varnish to give a protective coat.

MOULD-MAKING

Fimo can be used to make a mould. If you have something with a raised surface that you wish to copy, roll out a piece of fimo. Press the object into the fimo and lift it out, leaving an impression. Coins are very good for this. The fimo should then be baked to make a mould.

To make copies of your original, just press fimo into the mould and then lift out the shape. You may need to trim the shapes.

If you are using coins and wish to turn them into medallions, remember to make a hole in them with a skewer before baking.

ANIMAL SHAPES

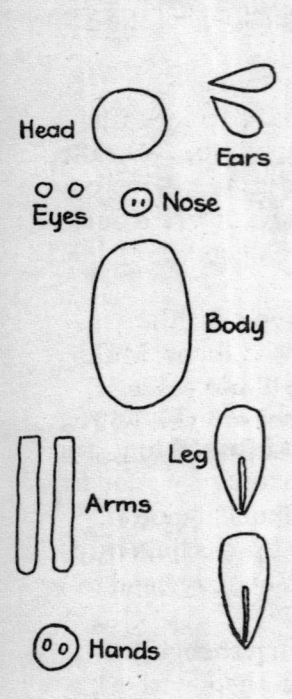

**Dinah Angel Pig

YOU WILL NEED
pink, blue and yellow fimo
1 pin
1 brooch back
strong glue

TO MAKE
1 Knead the pink fimo until it is soft.
2 Roll the shapes as shown.
3 Stick all the bits onto the body shape. Make holes in the nose and mark the trotters and hands with the pin.
4 Knead the yellow fimo and cut out a wing shape.
5 Stick the wing onto the back of the body, not with glue but by pushing it.
6 Make tiny balls of blue fimo and stick them in place for the eyes. Make holes in the centre to look like pupils.
7 Bake at 140 C (275 F. Gas Mark 1) for 15 minutes, and leave to cool.
8 Stick on the brooch back with strong glue.

**Flapper Pig

YOU WILL NEED
navy blue, pink, yellow and white fimo   1 pin   1 brooch back   glue

TO MAKE
1 Knead the navy blue fimo until it is a soft shape.
2 Knead pink, white and yellow fimol
3 Shape arms, head, nose, hands and leg in pink fimo. 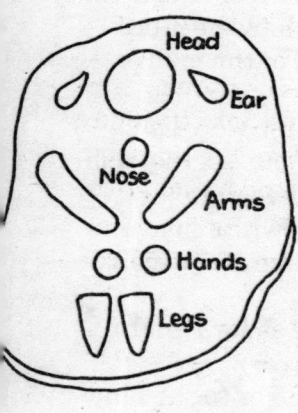
4 Make a thin roll of yellow for the belt of the dress. Stick it in place and mark the folds of the skirt with a pin.
5 Stick the body in place.
6 Make a fan shape from white fimo and stick in position. Mark it with a pin.
7 Make little balls of white fimo and stick on for the bead necklace.
8 Stick white fimo onto the bottom of the legs as shoes. Make a head band from a thin piece of white fimo with its own yellow rose.
9 Make blue eyes from tiny balls of blue fimo.
10 Bake at 140 C (275 F, Gas Mark 1) for 15 minutes. Then cool.
11 Glue the brooch back onto the pig.

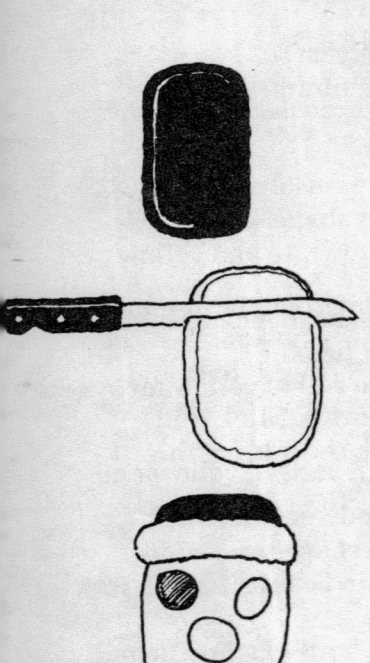

**Pig in Bed

YOU WILL NEED
mauve, white, red, pink, yellow and blue fimo
1 pin, 1 brooch back, glue

TO MAKE
1 Roll our an oval of blue fimo.
2 Roll out an oval of mauve fimo slightly bigger than the blue.
3 Trim the end of the mauve fimo.
4 Roll out small balls of blue, yellow and red fimo, and squash flat onto the mauve fimo.
5 Cut a strip of white fimo and stick onto the edge of the mauve fimo.
6 Make a head as for Dinah Angel Pig (see over).
7 Stick the head onto the blue background.
8 Add the mauve coverlet.
9 Make markings to decorate the coverlet with the pin.
10 Back at 140°C (275°F, Gas Mark 1) for 20 minutes. Then cool.
11 Glue on the brooch back.

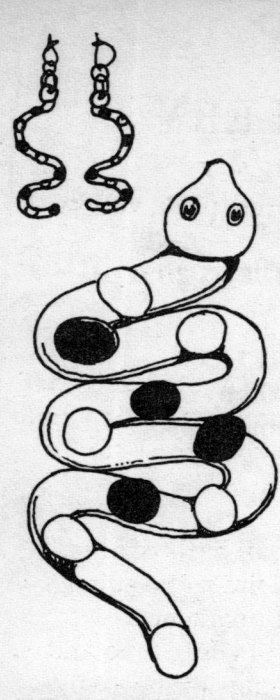

*Snakes

YOU WILL NEED
bright pink, yellow and dark green fimo

TO MAKE
1   Roll out the bright pink fimo into a long thin sausage about 10cm long.
2   Shape the fimo so that it looks like the body of a snake.
3   Make a ball of pink fimo and stick it on one end of the snake to form a head.
4   Make small balls of yellow and green fimo, and press them flat on top of the pink snake.

TO MAKE A BROOCH
1   Shape the snake by pushing the wiggles together.
2   Bake at 140°C (275°F, Gas mark 1) for 15 minutes.
3   Glue on a brooch pin.

TO MAKE EARRINGS
1   Make a hole in the snake's head.
2   Bake at 140°C (275°F, Gas Mark 1) for 15 minutes.
3   Thread a jump ring through the head of the snake, and an earring finding through the jump ring.

CHRISTMAS JEWELLERY

Use Christmas motifs such as puddings, trees, holly etc. to make brooches, badges and earrings.

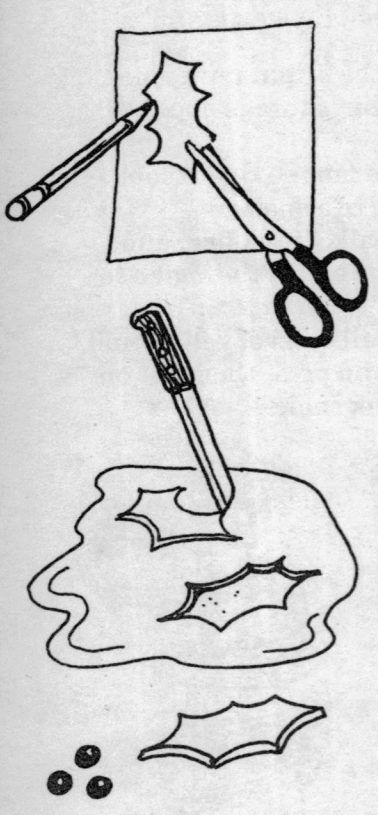

**Holly earrings and brooch

YOU WILL NEED
green and red fimo
pencil, paper and scissors
1 brooch back
2 earring findings
2 head pins
2 gold beads
rolling pin
a craft knife
strong glue

TO MAKE THE BASIC SHAPE
1   Draw 2 holly leaves on paper, one larger than the other. Cut them out. These are your templates.
2   Roll out the green fimo and place the template on top of it. cut out the holly shapes using the template as a guide.
3   Roll out three little balls of red fimo for each article of jewellery.

26

4 Stick one leaf on top of another and the berries on top of the leaves.

TO MAKE THE BROOCH
1 Bake the holly leaves and berries at 140°C (275°F, Gas Mark 1) for 15 minutes.
2 Glue on the brooch back.

TO MAKE EARRINGS
1 Make holes near the top of the leaves between the berries.
2 Bake at 140°C, (275°F, Gas Mark 1) for 10 minutes.
3 Thread the gold bead onto the head pin.
4 Put the pin through the berries so that the gold bead sits on top of them. Bend the back of the wire round some round-nosed pliers to form a loop.
5 Thread the loop onto the earring finding.

*Christmas pudding brooch

YOU WILL NEED
brown fimo
green fimo
red fimo
yellow fimo
white fimo
strong glue
brooch back
rolling pin

TO MAKE
1   Roll a piece of brown fimo in your hands until it forms a ball. Flatten the ball with the palm of your hand.
2   Roll a piece of yellow fimo as you did the brown and then flatten it. Once the ball is flattened cut out this shape.
3   Stick the yellow shape onto the brown.
4   Make a crescent of white fimo and stick it on the bottom of the pudding to form the dish.
5   Make small green leaves and red fimo berries, stick these into place.
6   Bake the pudding in the oven and when it is cool stick on the brooch back.

Christmas Pudding earrings

YOU WILL NEED
brown fimo
yellow fimo
green fimo
red fimo
white fimo
1 head pin
1 bead cup
2 small gold beads
1 jump ring
1 earring finding
with a loop
rolling pin

TO MAKE
1 Roll a ball of brown fimo, about the size of a marble, in your hand.
2 Using the rolling pin, roll out some yellow fimo until it is flat. This is the custard.
3 Cut a piece of yellow fimo in a very uneven circle and use it to cover the brown pudding. Make sure there is still some pudding showing.
4 Cut three tiny leaves from green fimo and add these to the top of the pudding.
5 Roll 2 tiny balls from the red fimo and stick these on top of the pudding.
6 Roll out some white fimo and cut a circle to make a plate. Put the pudding onto the plate and push firmly together.
7 Using the head pin make a hole through the pudding from the bottom to the top. Make the second earring as you did the first and then bake in the oven.
8 Thread the head pin onto the bead cup and then add the pudding. Thread on the 2 gold beads. Bend the head pin round to form a loop.
9 Thread the loop onto the jump ring and the earring finding.

Christmas Tree brooch

YOU WILL NEED
white fimo
green fimo
yellow fimo
pink fimo
red fimo
blue fimo
brown fimo
strong glue
brooch back
rolling pin

TO MAKE
1   Draw the christmas tree shape onto paper and cut it out to use as a template.
2   Roll out the green fimo, press the paper christmas tree shape on top and cut out the tree using a blunt kitchen knife.
3   From white fimo make a simple oblong doll shape. Drape yellow fimo hair on her head. Make pink hands and a mouth and blue eyes, press all these in place and then sit the doll on the top of the tree.
4   Cut a bucket shape from brown fimo for the bottom of the tree.
5   Mix pink, yellow and white fimo together to form a marbled effect and then roll a long snake. Drape this along the tree.
6   Make tiny balls of many colours and stick them into place.
7   Bake the brooch in the oven. When it is cold stick on the brooch back using a strong glue.

Beads

Beads can be made from almost anything and in this chapter we show you how to make some very cheap beads, how to string together beads, and how to work out the number of beads needed to make a necklace.

Find out how to weave with beads and how to decorate them.

There are sophisticated evening necklaces and zany necklaces you will want to wear almost before they're finished.

BEADS FROM PAPER

This is one of the easiest and cheapest ways of making beads. Use old birthday cards, magazines, wrapping paper or even newspaper to achieve different looks. You can use plain paper and paint the beads before varnishing.

The size of the beads can be varied according to the size of the triangle used.

YOU WILL NEED
paper or card
a pencil
a ruler
scissors
a knitting needle
glue (Copydex is good or a glue stick is easy)
plasticine
poster paints in lots of bright colours
clear nail varnish

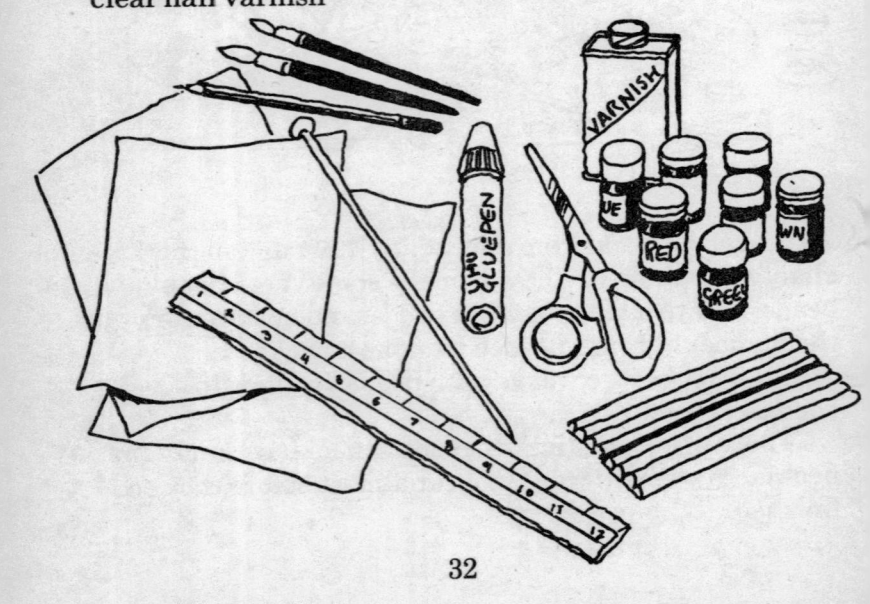

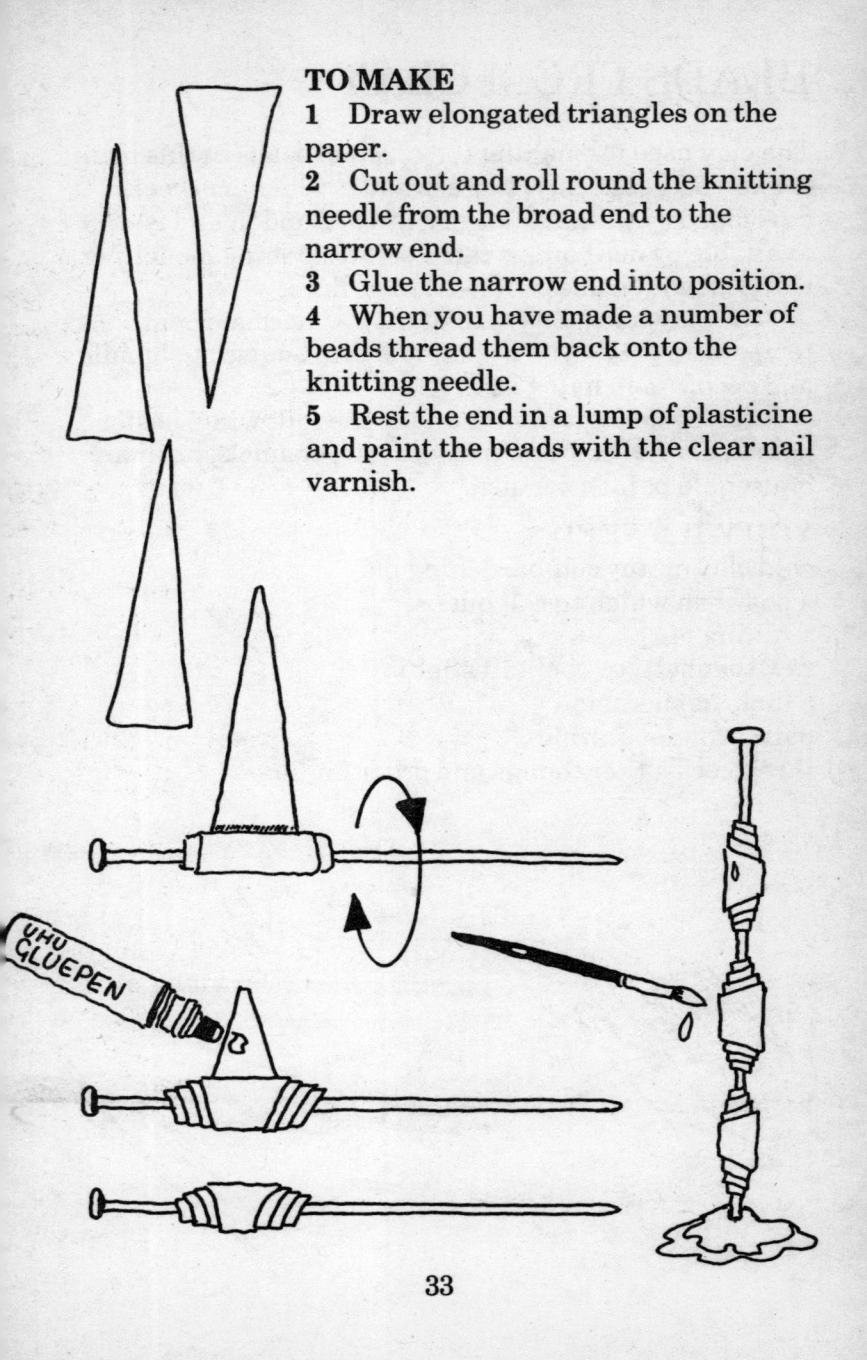

TO MAKE
1   Draw elongated triangles on the paper.
2   Cut out and roll round the knitting needle from the broad end to the narrow end.
3   Glue the narrow end into position.
4   When you have made a number of beads thread them back onto the knitting needle.
5   Rest the end in a lump of plasticine and paint the beads with the clear nail varnish.

BEADS FROM CLAY

The clay used for making the ceramic beads in this book is known as cold clay. It is a product which has been developed by Fulham Pottery Ltd of London and is available by mail order. It is a self-hardening modelling material which does not need to be fired.

The clay takes 2 days to harden at normal room temperature (17°C, 65°F), but it is firm enough to handle and decorate in half a day.

It can be decorated with any of the following: poster paints, acrylic colours, spray paints, enamels, ordinary household paints, varnish.

YOU WILL NEED
cold clay or any self-hardening clay
a board on which to roll out
a rolling pin
raw spaghetti or cocktail sticks
a lump of plasticine
paints for decorating
thread or leather thongs and other findings

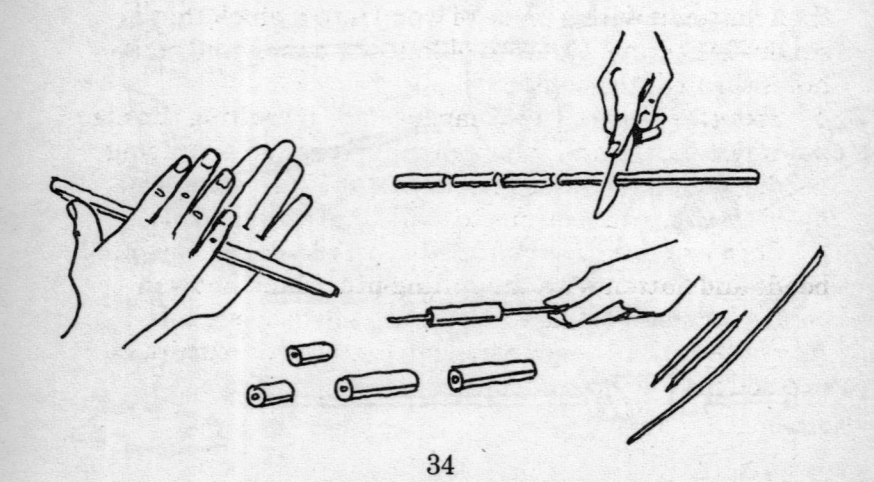

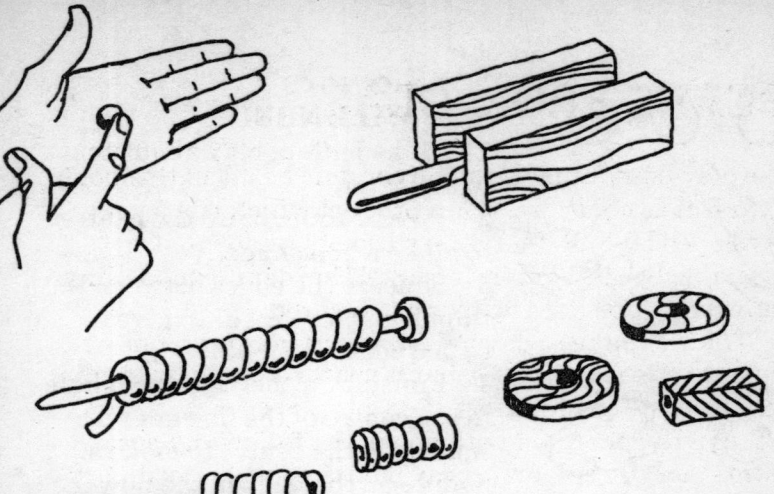

TO MAKE

1 Long beads With your hands, roll long pieces of clay on the board. Cut into lengths of equal size and make holes in each piece with a piece of spaghetti or a cocktail stick. If you need larger holes, use a knitting needle.

2 Round beads Make as for long beads, but once they are cut take each piece of clay and roll it in your hands to make a ball. Make a hole through each bead with a needle.

3 Square and rectangular beads Make a long coil, then flatten it with a piece of wood into a block that is square in section. Cut into oblongs or cubes, and make holes through the centre.

4 Tubular beads These can be made by rolling the clay flat on the board and then wrapping it round a knitting needle, pencil, or other cylinder. Make sure the edges overlap. Cut into sections to make individual beads.

5 Coin or medallion shaped beads Make as for round beads and flatten with the rolling-pin. Make holes in centre for small beads and near the top for pendants. Any of the above beads can have patterns or textures pressed into them to decorate them.

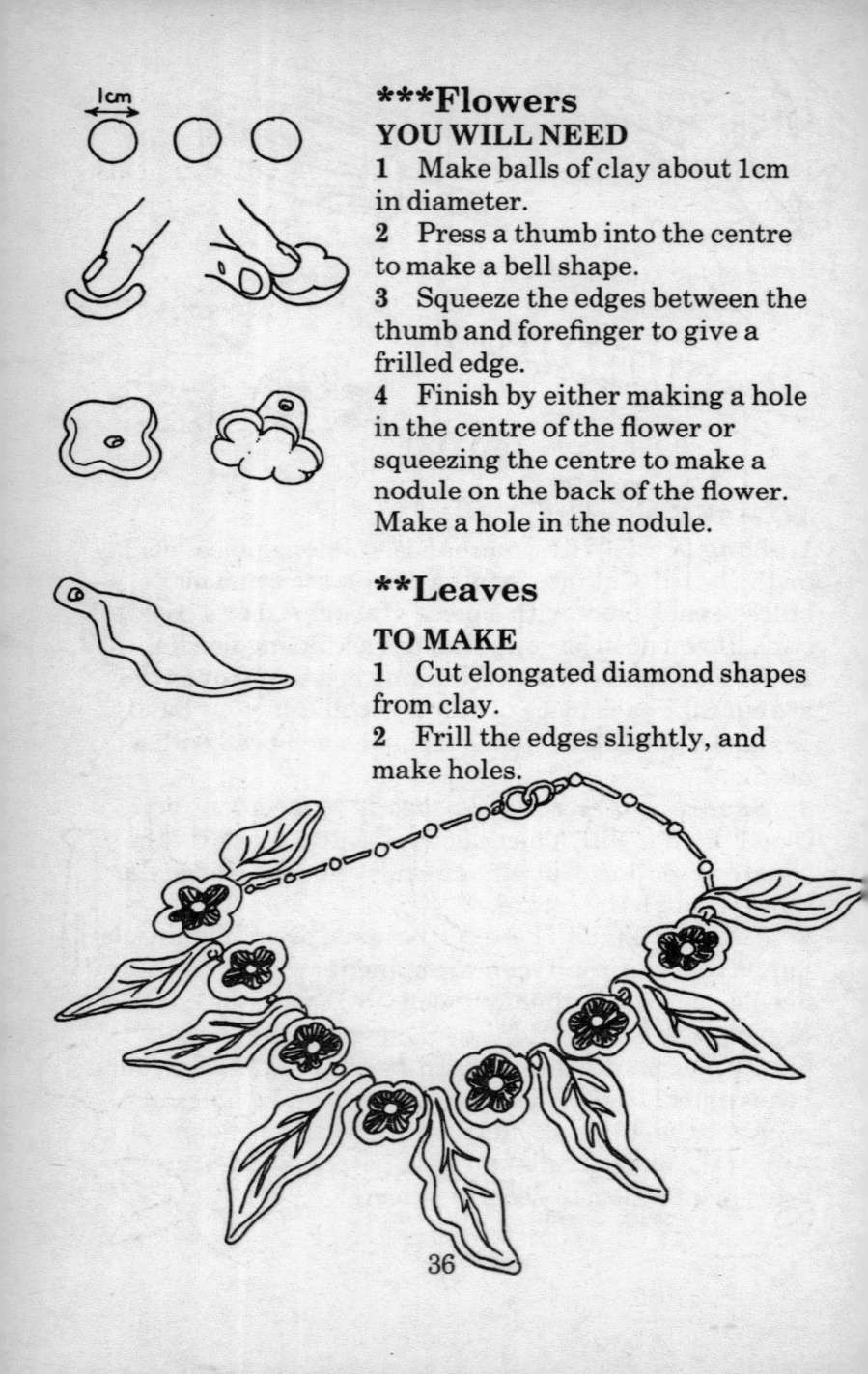

***Flowers
YOU WILL NEED
1   Make balls of clay about 1cm in diameter.
2   Press a thumb into the centre to make a bell shape.
3   Squeeze the edges between the thumb and forefinger to give a frilled edge.
4   Finish by either making a hole in the centre of the flower or squeezing the centre to make a nodule on the back of the flower. Make a hole in the nodule.

**Leaves

TO MAKE
1   Cut elongated diamond shapes from clay.
2   Frill the edges slightly, and make holes.

Other Shapes

Look in books for inspiration for simple stylized animals such as teddy bears, snakes, fruit etc. Don't forget to make a hole in the top of each shape. Keep the shapes fairly simple and add detail when decorating.

Finish a model with a coat of clear varnish. This will help to protect the shape.

BAKERS CLAY

Although this mixture is sometimes known as bread dough it is inedible because of the amount of salt added and the hardness that it is baked to. It is a very good clay substitute and you can use it to make beads and brooches.

YOU WILL NEED
3 cups plain flour
1 cup of salt
1 tsp glycerine (you can work without the glycerine but it makes it easier to work with. Buy this from the chemist)
1 cup water. (The size of the cup is unimportant as long as the same cup is used throughout.)

TO MAKE THE DOUGH
1   Sieve the dry ingredients into a bowl, add the glycerine.
2   Pour in the water, stirring thoroughly the whole time.

3 When the mixture is fairly stiff take it out and knead it as if making bread. If it is too dry add more water if it is too wet add some more flour.

This dough can be stored for a few days if wrapped in cling film or an airtight plastic container.

TO MAKE BEADS
Roll the dough into balls and thread on a skewer to cook in the oven. Decorate with paint and varnish after cooking.

TO MAKE PENDANTS AND BROOCHES
Roll the dough out as for ordinary pastry. Use miniature pastry cutters or mould your own shapes. Stick on brooch backs after cooking and decorating. Don't forget to make a hole near the top of a pendant before baking.

DECORATING BEADS

What to decorate:
* Papier mâché beads.
* Wooden beads – these can be bought in a non-varnished unpainted state.
* Pasta beads.   * Ceramic beads.

What you need

Beads and Badges can be painted with almost anything. Poster paints are ideal as they are opaque and dry quickly. As they have a chalky finish when dry, finish by coating with clear varnish after the paint has dried. Inks have a translucent quality, as does wood stain. Use these on wooden beads if you wish the grain to show.

Small tins of brightly-coloured enamel paints may be obtained from toy, model and craft shops. These take a long time to dry, but give strong colours and a shiny finish. Permanent markers are an easy way of applying detail to beads.

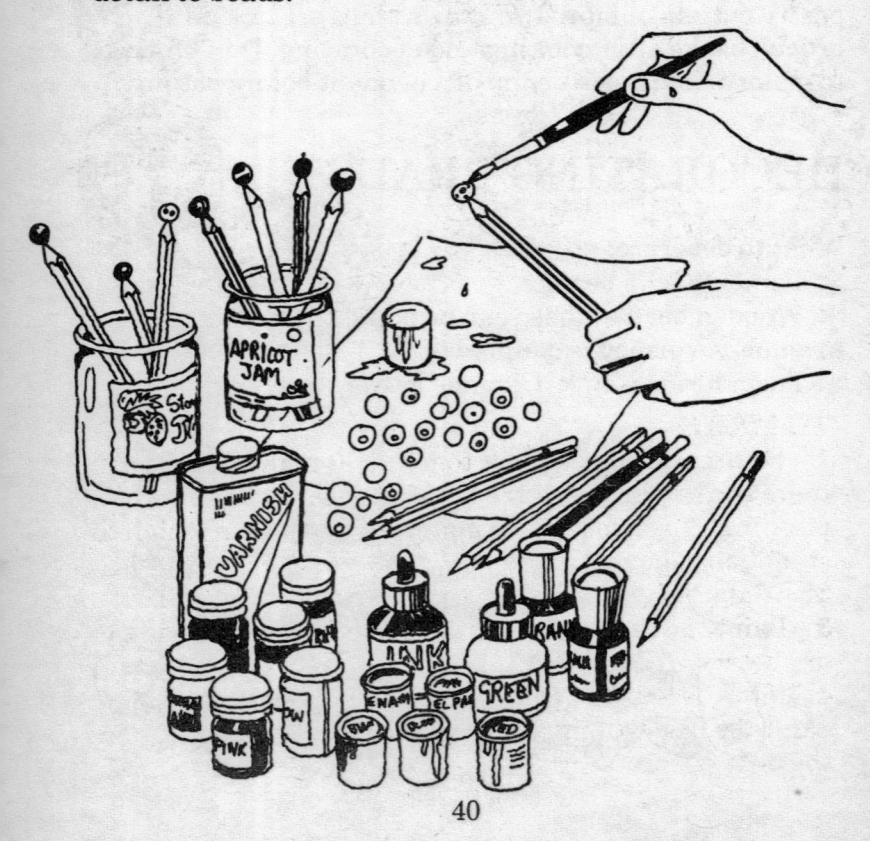

TO MAKE

1 Before starting, collect together as many pencils as there are beads. These are to balance the beads on whilst painting. Also, you need a couple of jam jars in which to stand the pencils.
2 Wedge a bead onto the pointed end of the pencil.
3 Paint the first coat onto the bead. Leave the bead to dry between coats.
4 If the bead is to have many colours and patterns, paint the first colour onto every bead before starting on the next colour.

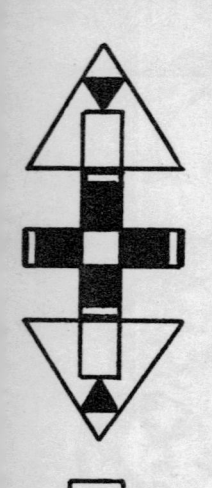

BEAD WEAVING

Bead weaving is very easy and it is possible to produce incredible results without buying expensive equipment. the strips of beads can be used as necklaces or sewn onto belts, bangles or clothes.

Most American Indian beadwork was traditionally made by the following method. Before starting your piece of weaving look at traditional Indian motifs for design inspiration. The designs will look best made up in bright opaque rocaille beads.

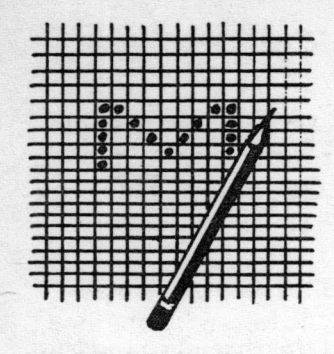

To begin with, draw your design on graph paper with one square equal to one bead.

Weaving beads is similar to weaving cloth in that there are warp threads (running from top to bottom) which are held in tension on the loom, and weft threads (passing from side to side) which carry the beads. The weft threads are woven in and out of the warp threads.

Bead looms can be bought from Hobby Horse (see p96) and other good craft shops. They come with a spring at each end to separate the warp thread, and rollers to wind on the work.

You could make your own bead loom by using the base of a strong cardboard box. Notch the edge at intervals of 2mm. Wind the thread – as tightly as you can – round the box and through the notches.

The best thread to use is a buttonhole thread as this is very strong.

Note: You need one thread more than the number of beads in the width of the design, e.g. for 6 beads use 7 warp threads.

***Weaving

YOU WILL NEED
rocaille beads (the quantity depends on what you are weaving)
beading needle (this is a long very fine needle)
bead loom
beading thread

TO MAKE
1   Thread the loom – that is, wind the thread round the box and through the notches.
2   Cut another piece of thread as long as possible without getting it in a knot.
3   Thread one end of this onto a beading needle and tie the other end onto the first warp thread at the beginning. This is now the weft thread.
4   Put the correct number of beads (the same number of beads as there are gaps between threads) onto the weft thread.
5   Pass the needle and beads underneath the warp threads, and position the beads so that each bead is in a gap between the threads.

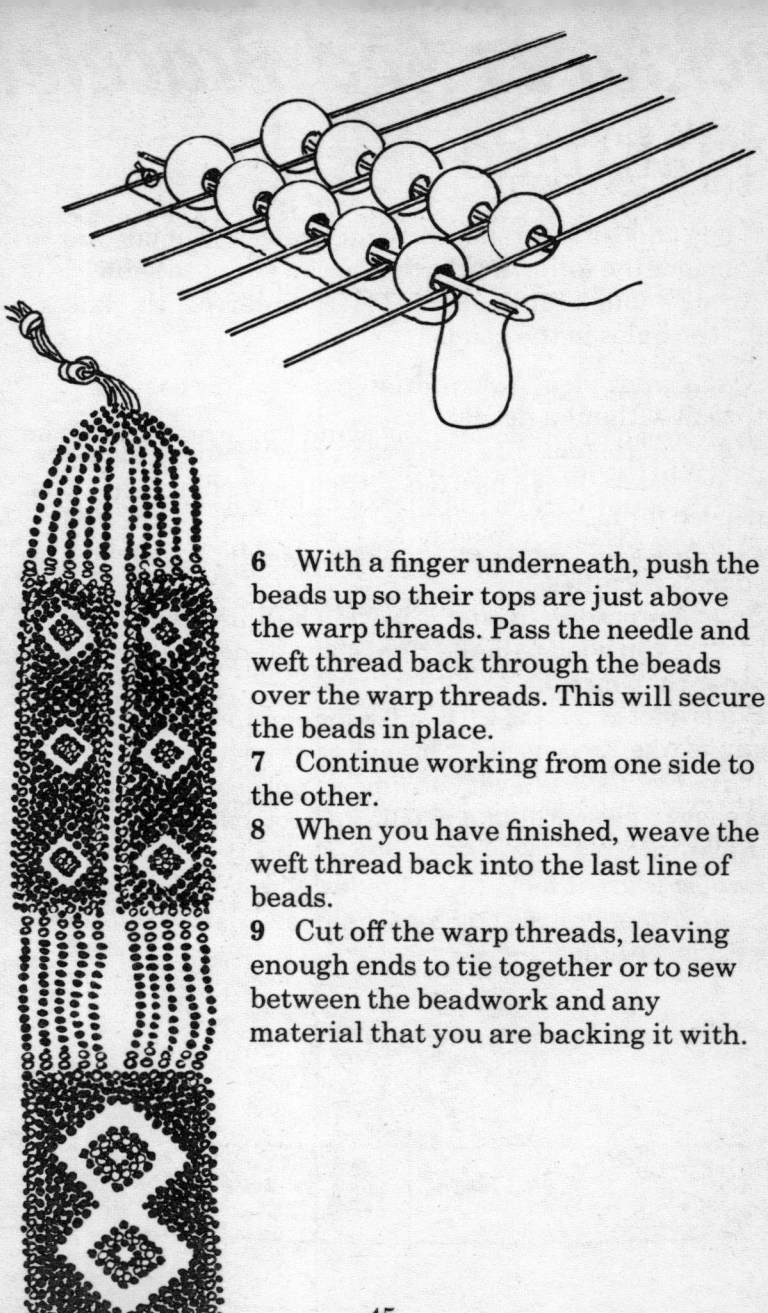

6 With a finger underneath, push the beads up so their tops are just above the warp threads. Pass the needle and weft thread back through the beads over the warp threads. This will secure the beads in place.
7 Continue working from one side to the other.
8 When you have finished, weave the weft thread back into the last line of beads.
9 Cut off the warp threads, leaving enough ends to tie together or to sew between the beadwork and any material that you are backing it with.

Necklaces And Bracelets

THREADING

When choosing threads for your beads it is important to consider the following: Is the thread going to show? Is it strong enough for the beads? Is it the correct thickness for the holes in the beads?

Nylon gut is ideal for children to use as it is easy to thread without a needle.
Tiger tail is steel wire covered in plastic and is ideal for heavy beads. It can be used without a needle. A crimp is needed for fastening tiger tail as it cannot be knotted.
Fine brass wire or *nylon thread* is ideal for fine beads such as rocailles.
Spun rayon covered wire is used in millinery work but is ideal if you wish to make rigid shapes with something other than metal.
Silver-plated wire use 0.6 or 0.8 for earrings. A thicker gauge like 1.5 is used for bracelets or necklaces.
Waxed terylene is a very strong all-purpose thread which is easy to use without a needle and comes in various thicknesses.
Rubber is great for junk or fun jewellery.
Leather thongs are good for ethnic jewellery or beads with large holes.

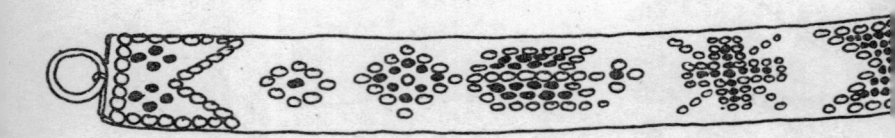

The necklaces and bracelets in this section are patterns to start you off in designing jewellery. The choice of beads and the way they are put together is a matter of personal taste and not something to be dictated.

Look in museums for inspiration. Go round the shops and adapt what you see to suit you. Look at jewellery worn in paintings, on the stage, in films and in books, as well as at what other people wear.

Before stringing a necklace, put different beads on a table next to one another. Do the beads look good all the same size? Do they look better interspersed with smaller beads? Do you want to have a large bead as a centre piece? Try contrasting colours, textures and sizes, for example wood and metal.

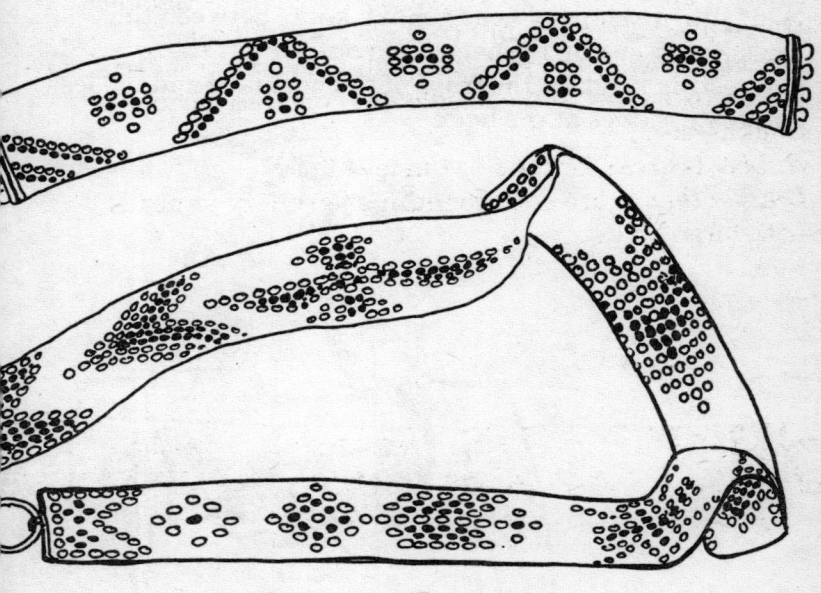

Helpful hints

✱ If you are making a necklace with a large central bead, put a needle on both ends and work from the middle outwards.

✱ When making a necklace with pieces hanging from it, attach the pieces to jump rings. They will hang better.

✱ Work a choker from the centre outwards, as the fit is crucial. You may then add or subtract pieces from both sides.

✱ To calculate the number of beads required, work out the number of beads that fit a 1cm length and multiply this by the total length required.

✱ As a guide:
a short necklace is 38-50cm long
a medium necklace is 60cm-70cm long
a long necklace is 80cm-125cm long

✱ If you are short of beads, make knots between the ones you are using to space them out. Or put the interesting beads at the front of the necklace and the less interesting ones at the back.

PROJECTS

Fish necklace

YOU WILL NEED

wooden beads
turquoise washers
small yellow and small blue beads
2 yellow and 1 blue fish
yellow and turquoise coco tusks
2 French crimps
1 jump ring
1 bolt ring tiger tail
3 jump rings for the fish.

TO MAKE

1 Thread the jump rings onto the fish.
2 Working from the centre of the necklace thread on fish and coco tusks separated by small beads.
3 For the back of the necklace thread alternately small yellow beads and turquoise washers.
4 Finish with a French crimp (see p17) and the bolt ring on one end and the jump ring on the other.

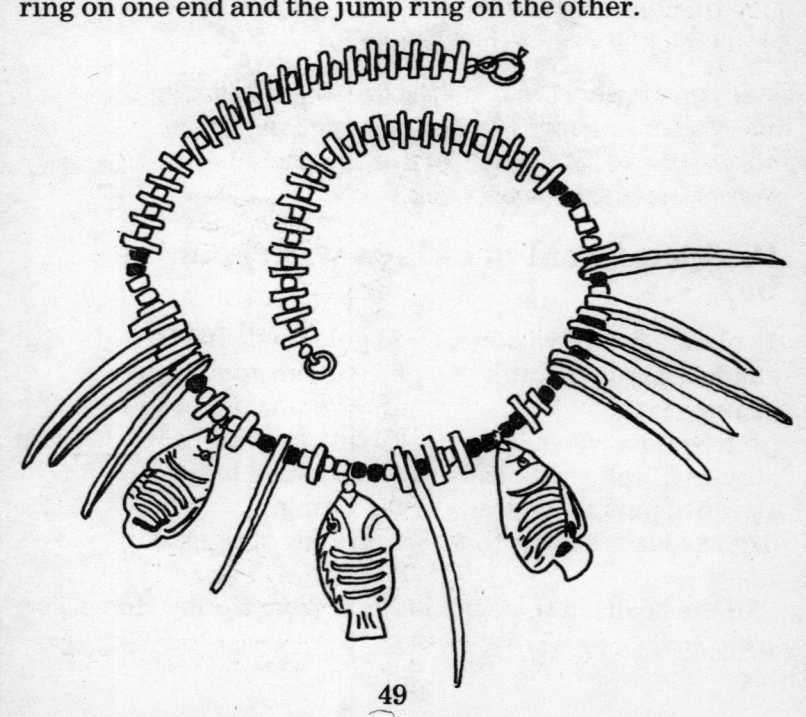

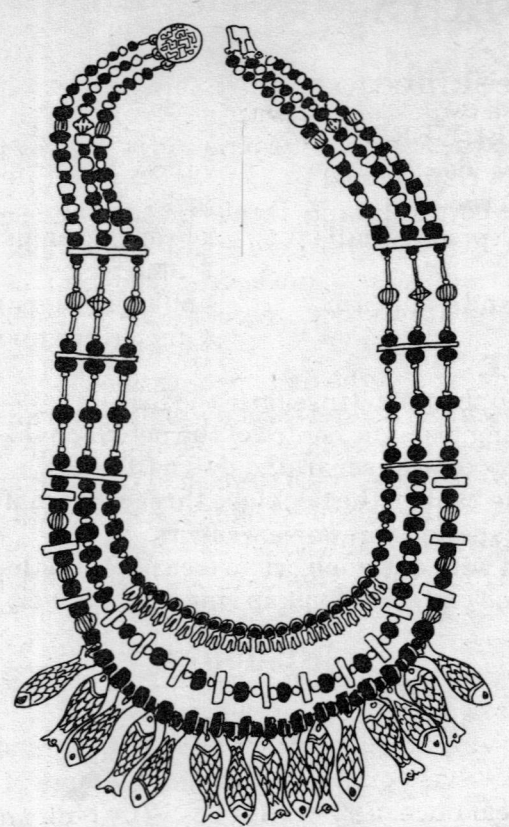

Pink and gold necklace with spacing bars

15 plastic fish in various shades of red and pink
15 jump rings
pink wooden washers
string of pink 4mm beads
string of pink 6mm beads
6 gold spacer bars with 3 holes
24 gold bugle beads
58 × 3mm gold beads
18 × 7mm gold beads
19 tiny gold bell caps
clasp with 3 loops for fastening
3 strands of tiger tail

(All the beads in this necklace are from Hobby Horse, see p96).

TO MAKE

Work from the middle outwards.

1   Thread the fish onto the jump rings, half by their tails and half by their noses.
2   On the bottom strand, thread on 4mm and 6mm beads and a fish. Repeat until there are 31 beads in all.
3   To each add a 7mm gold bead, a 6mm pink bead and a washer. Repeat this twice more. Finish with a 6mm pink bead.
4   Thread through the first spacing bars.
5   On the middle strand thread a 4mm, 6mm and 4mm bead, followed by a washer. Repeat until their are 9 washers. Add a 4mm and a 6mm bead to either side until there are 6 × 6mm and 6 × 4mm beads. Thread either end through the middle hole in the spacing bars.
6   On the top strand, alternate 20 × 4mm pink beads with the tiny gold bell caps. To either end add 1 × 3mm gold bead and 1 × 6mm pink bead until there are 5 pink beads. Thread each side through the top holes in the spacing bars.
7   Add the following to either end of each of the 3 strands: 1 × 6mm pink, 1 × 3mm gold, 1 bugle, 1 × 3mm gold. Repeat once. Finish with 1 × 6mm pink and thread through a spacing bar. Then add 1 × 4mm pink, 1 × 3mm gold, 1 bugle, 1 × 3mm gold, 1 × 6mm gold, 1 × 3mm gold, 1 bugle, 1 × 3mm gold, 1 × 4mm pink, through a spacing bar.
8   Add the following to all the strands: 1 × 6mm pink, 1 × 4mm pink 5 times, followed by 1 × 6mm gold, 1 6mm pink. Finished with 10 × 4mm pink beads.
9   Knot all the strands onto the clasp. Thread the loose ends back through the last through beads.
10 Cut any loose ends of thread with tin snips.

Dice bracelet

You can buy plastic dice with ready drilled holes. These can simply be made into a necklace or bracelet.

YOU WILL NEED
5 blue dice
5 red dice
13 small blue wooden beads
2 small yellow wooden beads
shirring elastic

TO MAKE
1 Thread 1 blue, 1 yellow, 1 blue bead onto the shirring elastic.
2 Thread on 1 blue dice, 1 blue bead, 1 red dice, 1 blue bead until you have used all the dice.
3 Thread on 1 blue, 1 yellow, 1 blue bead.
4 Knot the two ends of the shirring elastic together.

PUTTING ON THE GLITZ!

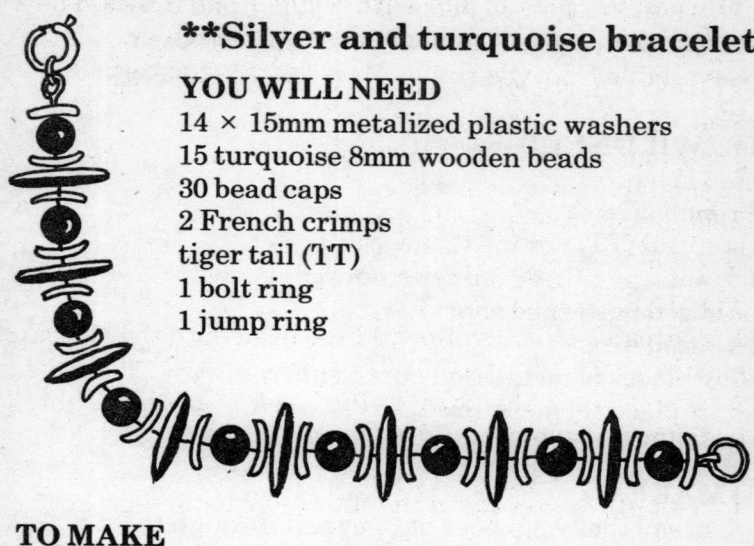

**Silver and turquoise bracelet

YOU WILL NEED
14 × 15mm metalized plastic washers
15 turquoise 8mm wooden beads
30 bead caps
2 French crimps
tiger tail (TT)
1 bolt ring
1 jump ring

TO MAKE
1   Thread one end of the TT through a French crimp. Then take the TT through the loop in the bolt ring and back through the French crimp.
2   Squeeze the French crimp tight with the flat-nosed pliers. The TT should now be held tight.
3   Thread on 1 bead cup, one bead, one bead cup, one metalized washer. Fig 1. Repeat until all the beads are threaded.
4   Finish as you started off using a French crimp, and this time a jump ring.

Idea
Use more beads and make a matching necklace.

Turquoise and silver Egyptian necklace.

This is a sophisticated piece of jewellery and it would make an ideal present for a grown up. (All those beads are available from the Hobby Horse catalogue, see p96).

YOU WILL NEED
fluted clasp
2 French crimps
1 tiger tail (TT) cut into 2 pieces
78 × 4mm metalized (silver-coloured) beads
4 oxidized patterned short barrels
8 oxidized urns
2 long pieces of metallized curved horn
2 short pieces of metallized curved horn
1 medallion with 3 holes at the back

TO MAKE
1 Thread the two pieces of tiger tail through the top and bottom holes of the medallion.
2 Working from the middle outwards, thread 8 × 4mm silver metallized beads on the bottom thread. Repeat on the other side of the centre medallion.

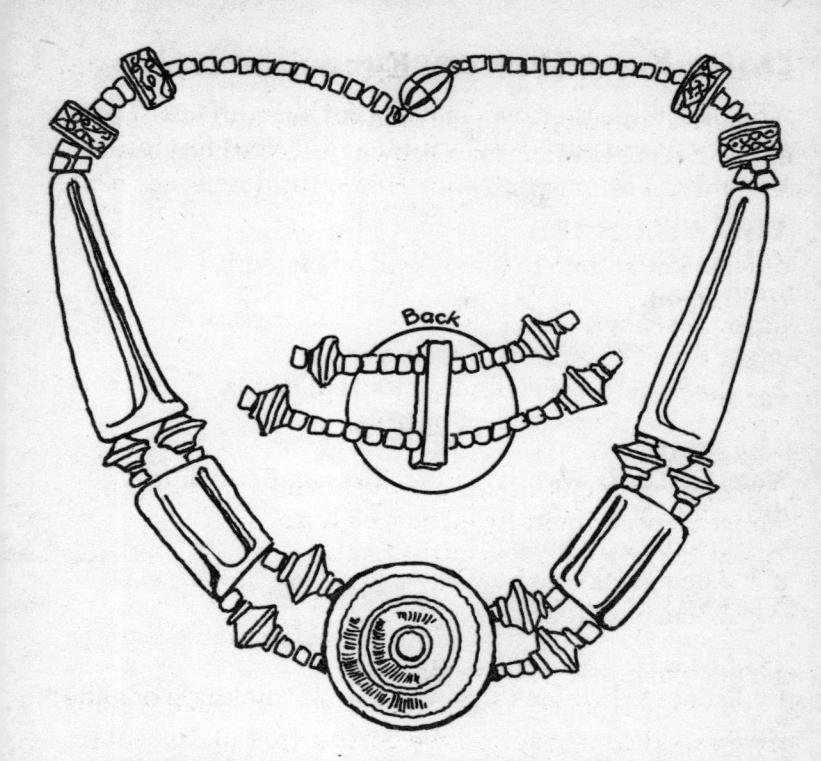

3 On the top thread, working from the middle outwards, thread 4 × 4mm beads.

4 Thread onto the end of each piece of TT, 1 urn and 1 × 4mm beads.

5 Thread the two threads through the short pieces of curved horn.

6 Now add onto each thread 1 × 4mm bead and 1 urn.

7 Thread onto both ends the long piece of curved horn.

8 On either side, thread on one bead to the top piece of TT and two beads to the bottom piece. Bring the threads together and thread on a patterned barrel.

9 On either side, thread on 3 × 4mm metallized beads, 1 short patterned barrel and 16 × 4mm beads.

10 Finish with the French crimps and barrel fastening.

Dotty Fimo Bow necklace

You can make the bows in different sizes and use them for all sorts of purposes by adding different findings to them.

YOU WILL NEED
one packet of fimo in black, and one in white
rolling pin
knife
ruler
varnish

The bows
Note: All the bows are made in the same way but in different sizes.
4 × 7cm brooch bows
2 × 4.5cm necklace bows
1 × 2.5cm earring bows

TO MAKE
1 Roll out the black fimo to an even thickness of about 3mm.
2 Cut out an appropriately sized strip in the main colour.
3 Make tiny dots by rolling tiny balls of white fimo and sticking these onto the bow.
4 Using your thumb and forefinger, pinch in the bow rectangles at the centre. Then, from the contrasting fimo, cut narrow strips for the centre of the necklace bows.
5 Wrap the strip around the centre of each bow, joining the ends together at the back.
6 For necklace bows. Use a head pin to make a hole through the centre from top to bottom.
7 Bake the bows in a pre-heated oven at 140°C, (275°F, Gas Mark 1) for 10-15 minutes. Leave to cool.

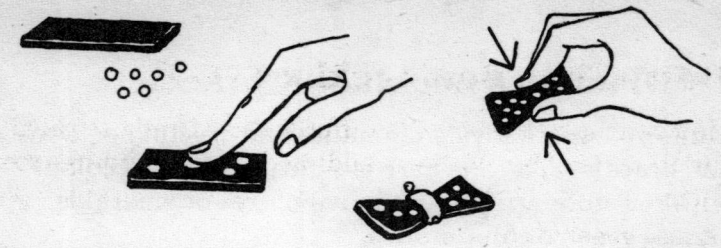

The necklace

YOU WILL NEAD
5 black and white necklace bows
small black and white wooden beads
tiger tail
clasp
french crimp
flat-nosed pliers
round-nosed pliers

TO MAKE
1   Thread one crimp onto the tiger tail, then take the tiger tail through the loop of the clasp and back through the crimp. Squeeze the crimp with the flat-nosed pliers to close.
2   Thread on black and white beads.
3   Thread a tiny bead cup onto a head pin and then thread this through the holes in the bow. Using round-nosed pliers, bend the top of each pin into a loop. Hook this loop onto the necklace.

***Diamante necklace & bracelet

Make yourself a lovely diamante and crystal necklace and bracelet. The one here is a natural crystal colour with red stones. If you prefer sapphires or emeralds, choose green or blue stones.

The beads are from Janet Coles' mail order catalogue and the correct codes are given (see p96 for address).

**FOR THE NECKLACE
YOU WILL NEED**
16 CR26 red stones
1 CR44 pear drop crystal
48 x 4mm crystals
14 x 5mm red crystal beads
1 clasp
2 French crimps
1 tiger tail (TT)
1 pair of flat-nosed pliers

TO MAKE
1 Thread the tiger tail through one French crimp and through the loop on one side of the clasp.
2 Pass the thread back through the crimp, and squeeze with the flat-nosed pliers to close the crimp and secure the tiger tail.
3 Thread on 1 red crystal bead and 1 × 4mm bead, repeat 6 more times.
4 Thread on 1 × 4mm bead, add 1 red stone and 2 × 4mm crystal beads.
5 Repeat until you have 8 red stones with 2 crystal beads on the side of each. Finish with 2 crystal beads and thread on the pear drop.
6 Work from the centre of the necklace so that it looks like the other side and finish with the crimp and the other wise of the clasp.

FOR THE BRACELET YOU WILL NEED

1 pear drop crystal
4 CR26 red crystal stones
2 CR20 crystal stones
2 × 6mm crystal beads
4 × 5mm red crystal beads
16 × 4mm crystal beads
tiger tail
2 French crimps
1 jump ring
1 bolt ring
1 pair flat-nosed jewellers pliers

TO MAKE

1 Join the tiger tail onto the bolt ring through the French crimp as you did for the necklace.
2 Thread on a 6mm crystal bead followed by 3 × 4mm crystal beads, 1 red bead, 1 CR20 crystal stone, 1 red bead, 1 × 4mm crystal bead, 1 red stone, 2 × 4mm crystal beads, 1 red stone, 2 × 4mm crystal beads and a pear drop.
3 Work the rest of the bracelet, so that it mirrors the half you have just done and finish off with a jump ring and French crimp.

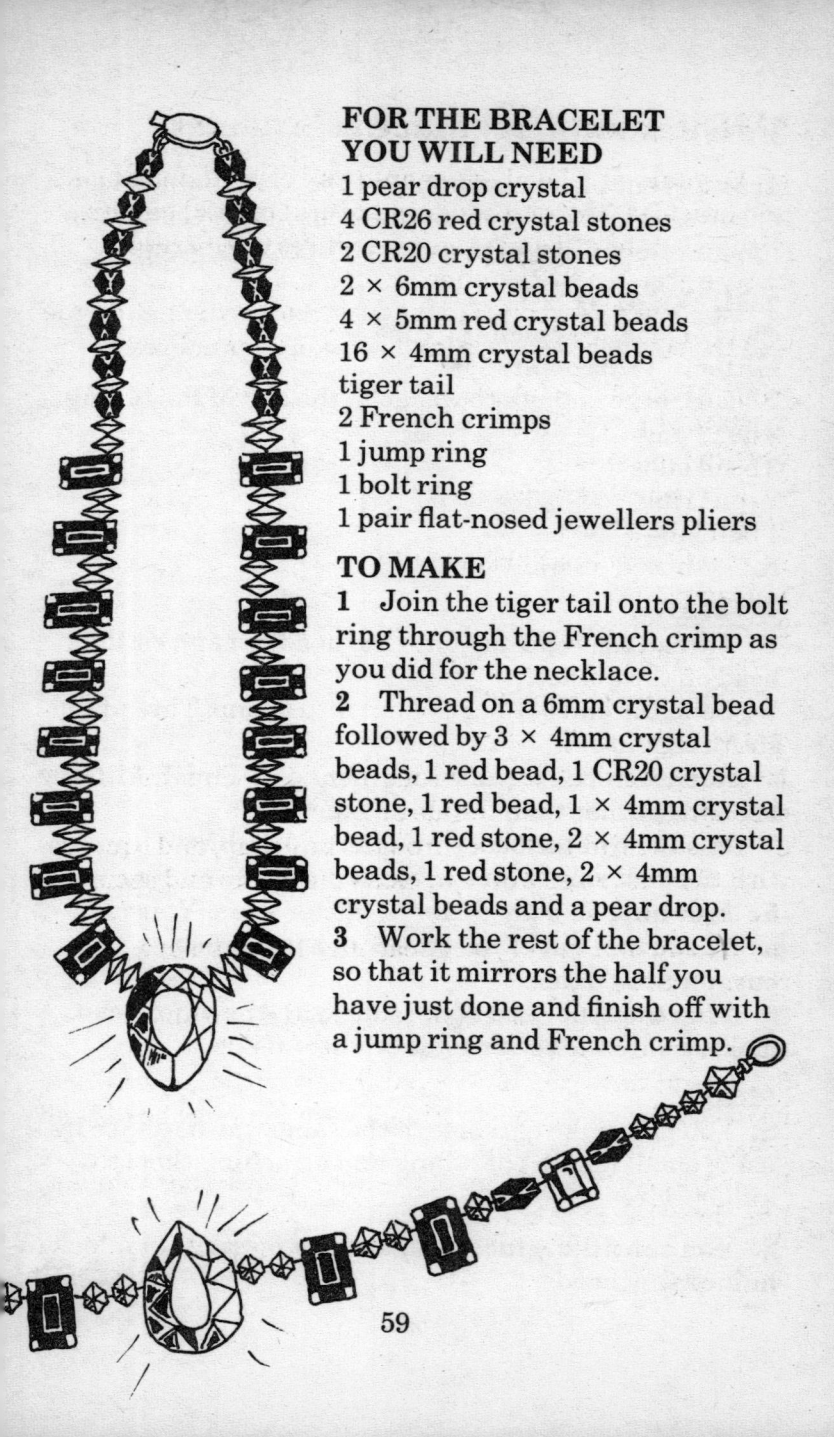

Fairy necklace

Transparent plastic syphoning tube is available in most hardware stores or plumbers merchants and can make fun jewellery filled with a variety of things.

YOU WILL NEED
45cm of plastic syphoning tube
glitter or glitter stars
2 beads large enough to wedge in the end of the tubing
2 head pins
2 bead cups
1 split ring
1 bolt ring
round-nosed pliers.

TO MAKE
1   Thread the bead cup onto the head pin and sit the bead on top of that.
2   Bend the end of the head pin into a loop. Thread the split ring onto it.
3   Repeat steps 1 and 2 with other bead. Finish with the bolt ring rather than the split ring.
4   Push one of the beads into the end of the tubing so that the bolt ring is on the outside.
5   Fill the tube with glitter or glitter stars. You can make a funnel out of the corner of a paper bag or envelope to do this.
6   Plug the other end of the tube with the other bead, making sure the split ring is on the outside.

Ideas

✱ You can make earrings in the same way as above by using small lengths of tubing and attaching them to kidney wires.

✱ You can fill the tube with a secret message or a lock of hair or tiny beads.

Earrings

Before you start making earrings, find something with tiny compartments to keep all your findings in. An ice cube tray is ideal.

0.4mm and 0.6mm wire are more commonly used in earring making. The 0.6mm holds its shape better than the 0.4mm.

*A hanging earring

YOU WILL NEED
1 head pin
a bead cup
enough beads to fit onto the head pin.
a clip-on earring finding with a loop or a kidney wire
round-nosed pliers

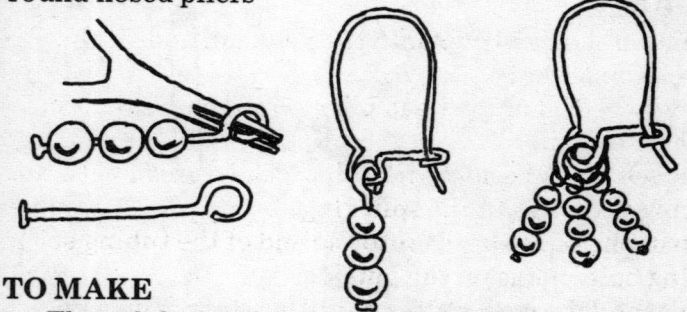

TO MAKE
1 Thread the bead cup onto the head pin, so that it looks like a saucer.
2 Thread on the beads, and leaving 6mm of wire at the end.
3 Grasp the spare wire with the round-nosed pliers and bend it into a loop so that it touches the shaft of the pin.
4 Adjust the loop with the pliers so the wire hangs from the centre of the loop.
5 Attach the loop to the bump in the kidney wire, or to the loop of the ear clip.
6 Close all the loops with the round-nosed pliers.

Variations

✶ Hang 2 or 3 pins of different lengths from one earring loop. It is a good idea to hang these from a jump ring and attach the jump ring to the finding.

✶ Make an earring using an eye pin. Then hang a large stone or bead from a bail attached to the eye.

✶ Use a spacer bar – a patterned piece of wire – instead of a pin for a prettier effect.

✶ Bend wire into triangles, spirals or zigzags for zany earrings.

✶ Use a perforated disc clip (this looks a little like a miniature colander) and sew tiny rocaille beads onto it. Then clip the disc onto an earring base.

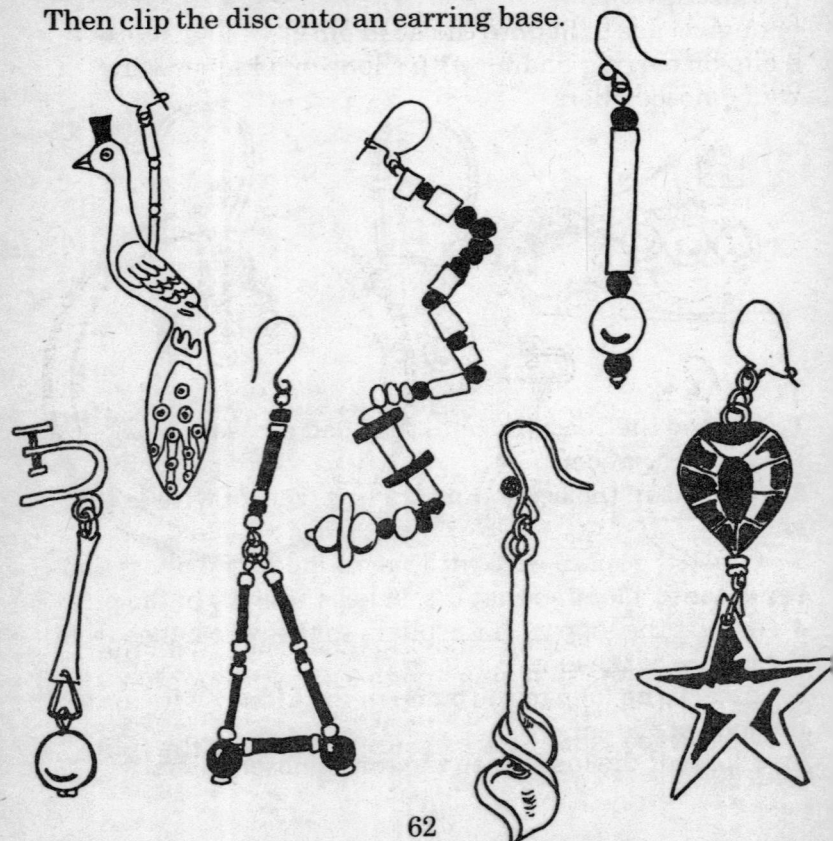

HOOPS

You can make earrings and bangles from the most unlikely household items.

Curtain ring earrings

YOU WILL NEED
2 large curtain rings with metal, plastic or wooden eyelets. Feel the weight of them before you start, as you don't want them to be too heavy to hang from your ears.
2 jump rings
Either 2 screw-on earclips with a hanging loop (for non pierced ears) **or** 2 Kidney wires (for pierced ears)
flat-nosed pliers

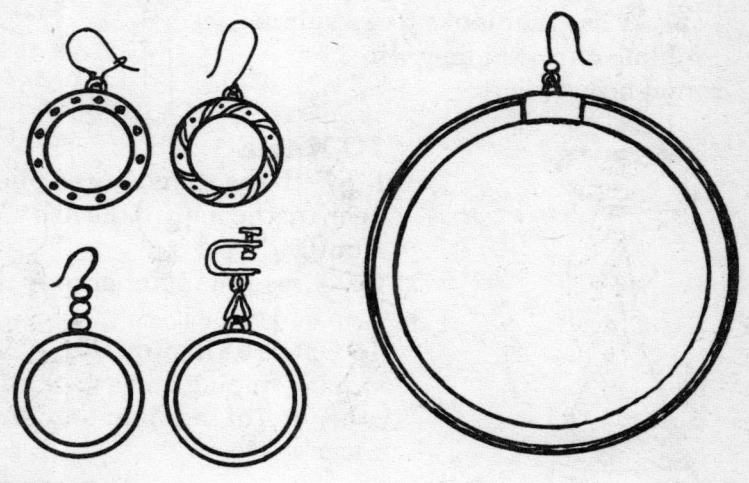

TO MAKE
1 Work on one earring first and then repeat with the second. Open the split ring and thread it through the eyelet on the curtain ring.
2 Thread the kidney wire or earclip through the split ring, and then close it.

ZOO EARRINGS

For each of the earrings below, the materials given make up *one* earring only. If you want a pair, double the quantities!

You can buy lots of different animals, birds, fish and insects from bead shops. Some of these come ready painted and others are left plain so that you can decorate them yourself.

Fish Earring

YOU WILL NEED
1 wooden painted fish with a loop at its mouth
1 spacer bar that looks like a spinner
1 folding clip or kidney wire
round-nosed pliers

TO MAKE
1   With the round-nosed pliers, open up the loop of the fish mouth.
2   Thread the spinner onto the loop and close it.
3   Open the loop on the earring finding and attach the other end of the spinner to it. Close the loop.

Tiger Earring

YOU WILL NEED
1 wooden tiger with a hole through its middle
1 gold-coloured head pin
1 gold-coloured bead cup
1 gold-coloured spacer bar
1 earring finding
wire cutters
round-nosed pliers

TO MAKE
1   Thread the bead cup onto the head pin.
2   Thread the pin through the body of the tiger so that the belly rests on the bead cup.
3   Cut the pin so there is just enough to make a loop but no more.
4   Make the loop but do not close it.
5   Thread the spacer bar onto the loop and close it.
6   Open the loop on the earring finding and thread on the spacer bar, close the loop.

Sea horse earring

YOU WILL NEED
1 sea horse
1 jump ring
1 earring finding

TO MAKE
1   Open the loop on the sea horse and thread on the jump ring,
close the loop.
2   Open the loop on the earring finding and thread on the jump ring,
close the loop.

FLOWERS

Glass rose earring

YOU WILL NEED
1 glass rose with a loop
1 S-shaped jump ring
1 earring finding

TO MAKE
1   Thread the rose onto one end of the S.
2   Thread the finding onto the other end of the S.

Freesia earring

YOU WILL NEED
1 x 6mm crystal bead
4 x 3mm crystal beads
1 eye pin
3 head pins
1 pink three-pronged plaster flower shape
1 ear hook

TO MAKE
1   Thread 1 x 6mm, 1 x 3mm bead, then the flower shape onto the eye pin.
2   Make a loop on the other end of the eye pin and attach it to the loop of the ear hook.
3   Cut the head pins into different lengths.
4   Thread a 3mm bead onto each head pin.
5   Make a loop at the end of each head pin and attach each of these to the loop under the flower.

DANGLING EARRINGS

All red earring

YOU WILL NEED
1 long drop bead in red
1 bail
1 spacer bar
1 jump ring
1 head pin
1 bead cup
1 red plastic fasseted heart
2 red fasseted beads of different sizes
1 earring finding

TO MAKE
1   Thread the spacer bar onto the jump ring and hang the jump ring from the earring finding.
2   Thread the bead cup onto the head pin. Then thread the red heart and two beads on top of the heart. Make a loop at the end and hang from the jump ring.

Carmen Miranda earrings

This earring is inspired by a film star who used to wear turbans laden with exotic fruit.

YOU WILL NEED
3 long eye pins
1 short eye pin
2 bails
2 jump rings
1 small purple leaf
3 purple glass beads
5 green rocaille beads
3 green glass beads
1 green pea pod
7 red glass beads
1 orange plastic leaf
11 bright yellow rocailles
1 glass banana
13 blue lastic beads
2 blue wooden discs
1 blue glass leaf with its own loop
1 earring finding with a loop.

TO MAKE
1   Thread the purple leaf onto of the jump rings.
2   Thread the green pea pod onto a bail and then thread and eye pin onto the top of the bail and thread on the green beads.
3   Make a loop at the top of the eye pin.
4   Thread the orange leaf onto a jump ring and thread this onto an eye pin. Thread the red beads onto the eye pin and make a loop at the other end.
5   Thread the banana onto a bail and the bail onto an eye pin. Thread on the yellow beads and make a loop at the end.

6 Thread the blue leaf onto an eye pin and then thread on 4 beads, a blue washer, then 9 blue beads and finish with a blue washer. Make a loop in the end.
7 Thread the 3 purple beads onto the small eye pin and make a loop at the other end. Join one end of the loop to the earring finding, the other end to the large jump ring.
8 Add the other columns of beads and the single purple leaf onto the large jump ring.

Spun glass earring

You will need
1 spun glass twisted drop
1 jump ring
1 earring finding with loop

TO MAKE
1 Thread the drop onto the jump ring.
2 Thread the jump ring onto the earring finding.

Zigzag earring

YOU WILL NEED
sequins threaded onto some cotton
small black wooden beads and washers
white beads and washers
earring finding
10cm of fine gauge wire

TO MAKE
1 Thread a large white bead on the wire. Curl up the end of the wire to stop the bead falling off.
2 Thread on the beads and sequins, alternating black and white.
3 Make a loop at the top of the wire.
4 Bend the wire so that you form a zigzag pattern.
5 Thread onto the earring finding.

Red and white dangling earring

YOU WILL NEED
1 red fasseted bead
1 white bead cut like a lily tomato
1 red teardrop stone
3 bead cups
1 bail
1 earring clip with a loop
1 eye pin

TO MAKE
1   Thread the lily tomato bead onto the eye pin.
2   Then thread on the bead cup so it fits round the top of the lily tomato bead.
3   Thread on another bead cup, the opposite way round to the last one.
4   Thread on the red bead followed by the last bead cup so it fits over the top of the bead.
5   Make a loop at the top of the pin and thread onto the earring finding.
6   Thread the bail through the bottom loop and hang the red teardrop stone from it.

Sewing Jewellery

Bugs

YOU WILL NEED
Small squares of felt in red, black, purple and yellow
1 small safety pin for each brooch
a small piece of black lace
a scrap of shiny material and sequin waste
a few pieces of wadding, old tights or cotton wool for stuffing
small mug or cup
a piece of tailors' chalk

Ladybird brooch

To make

1   Draw round a cup or small mug with a piece of tailors' chalk onto the red felt, until you have a complete circle.

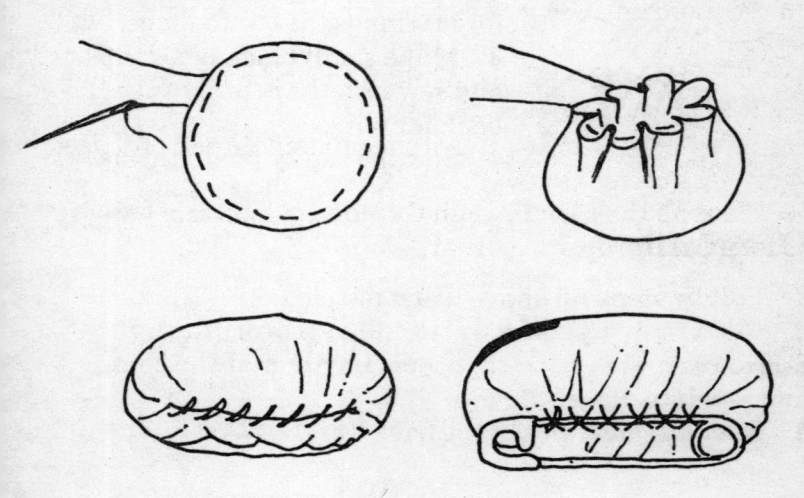

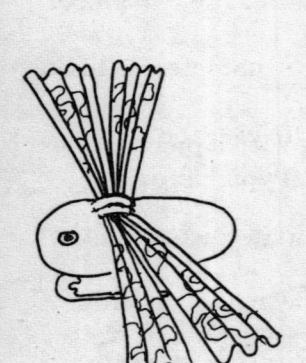

2 Cut out the circle and sew a line of running stitches as close to the edge as possible.
3 Gather up the running stitches and put some stuffing in the centre of the felt.
4 Pull the stitches up tight and finish off the ends.
5 Push the felt into a long shape. Oversew the gap to close it.
6 Cut the ladybird markings out of black felt and sew into position.
7 Sew the safety pin to the back of the lady bird to make the brooch.

Bee

1 Follow steps 1-5 above using black felt.
2 Cut thin strips of yellow felt for markings. Sew into place.
3 Make small black lace loops and sew into the centre of the back for wings.
4 Sew the safety pin to the back.

Dragonfly

1 Follow steps 1-5 above using purple felt.
2 Cut a strip of sequin waste and a strip of glittery fabric 10cm × 5cm. Gather them together at the centre and sew into place.
3 Sew the safety pin to the back.

Mouse brooch

YOU WILL NEED
a piece of small print fabric
approx 10cms square
a tiny piece of felt
1½ cotton wool balls
fabric glue (Copydex)
1 safety pin

TO MAKE
1. Cut 1 piece of the main shape in small print fabric.
2. Draw twice round a 2p on the felt. Cut the two pieces out. Cut 1 tail piece in felt.
3. Cut one of the felt circles across its diameter, to make a pair of ears.
4. Fold the main pattern piece in half, with the wrong side of the pattern on the outside.
5. Stitch down the dotted line.
6. Sew a line of running stitches around the base of the mouse.
7. Fill with the cotton wool and draw up the running stitches at the base of the mouse.
8. Stick the tail to the remaining felt circle. Stick the circle onto the bottom of the mouse.

9 Fold the semi-circles in half to make the ears. Oversew along the straight edge. Stitch into position near the top of the cone-shaped mouse.

10 You can finish by sewing a tiny bead at the point to make the nose.

11 Sew the pin onto the back seam

Idea
✽ Make a rabbit by the same method, but add a fluffy tail and pointed ears.

A baby in a bonnet brooch

This brooch is quite gruesome but great fun.

YOU WILL NEED
a piece of cotton wool about the size of a large marble
a piece of flesh-coloured tights
needle and some thread for sewing
pencil
12cm length of 1cm white lace
a circle of white cotton fabric about 3cm in diameter
a safety pin
scissors

TO MAKE
1   Cut a piece of tights material large enough to cover the cotton wool when it is double thickness.
2   Cover the cotton wool with a double thickness of material and tie with a knot.
3   With a pencil, dot in the eyes, nose, ears, and mouth.
4   Thread your needle, then double the thread and make a large knot.
5   Insert the needle from the back of the head, and sew on the eyes and other features. Pull the thread tight and knot at the back.
6   Gather the edge of the lace with a running stitch and pin into the edge of the head around the face. Sew into position.
7   Gather the edge of the circle of cotton fabric and sew over the back of the head and over the rough edges of the lace.
8   Attach the pin the back of the head.

Knitted And Woven Jewellery

Cord Wrapping

Why not use up all those tiny bits of wool that are too short to knit – make a necklace or a belt.

YOU WILL NEED
piping cord (this comes in various thicknesses; choose accordingly on how fat you want your necklace to be.)
scraps of wool
darning needle
sewing needle and thread

TO MAKE

1. Begin by wrapping 3cm from one end of the cord. Hold the end of the wool slightly down from the start and begin to wind the rope round the end of the wool.
2. Wind very tightly keeping the strands of the wool close together. Do not wind to the very end of the wool but leave at least 2cm.

3. To begin the next colour, hold the first piece of wool next to the second, and wind over both colours.
4. Continue adding colours until you're within 3cm of the end of the cord.
5. To make a complete circle, put the two ends of the cord together and sew with a few stitches.

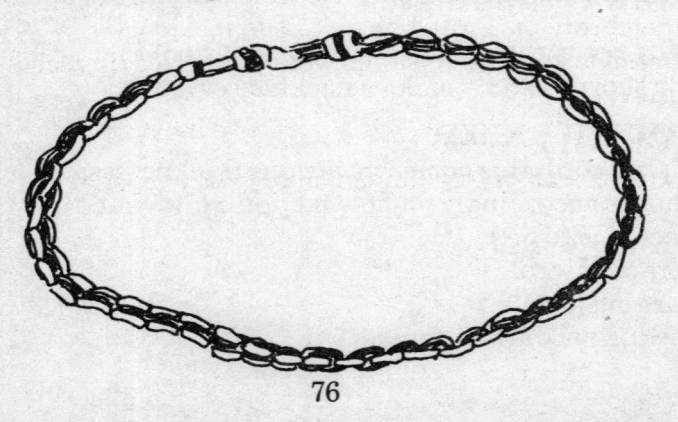

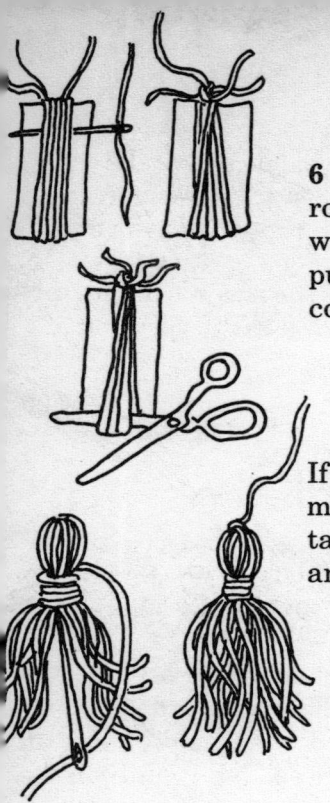

6 Cover the join by winding wool round it. Finish off by threading the wool through the darning needle and pulling it back through the completed section.

If you want to leave the ends free miss out steps 5 and 6 and make a tassel. Sew onto the ends using wool and a darning needle.

Woven cord armbands

These armbands can be made from any kind of sylko or embroidery thread. Six-skein embroidery thread is good because the weaving builds up reasonably quickly.

YOU WILL NEED
1 metre each of 3 colours of embroidery thread.
1 safety pin.
a pair of scissors

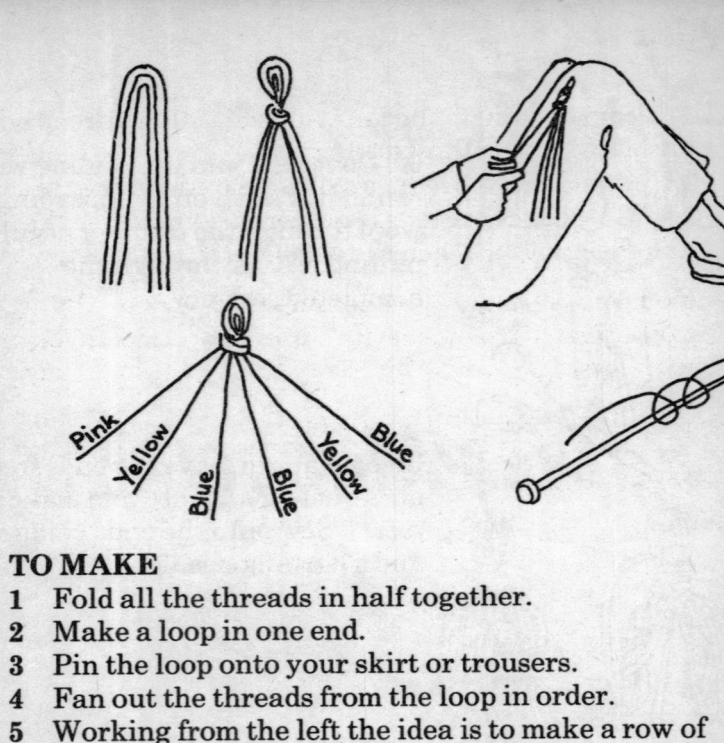

TO MAKE
1 Fold all the threads in half together.
2 Make a loop in one end.
3 Pin the loop onto your skirt or trousers.
4 Fan out the threads from the loop in order.
5 Working from the left the idea is to make a row of knots in one colour. Pick up thread No.1 (pink) in the right hand.
6 Pick up thread No.2 (yellow) in the left hand and make 2 pink half-hitch onto the yellow thread.
7 Drop the yellow thread and pick up thread No.3 (blue) and make two half-hitches in pink onto the blue thread.
8 Drop the blue thread and pick up thread No.4 (pink) and make two half-hitches in No.1 onto No.4.
9 Carry on using the thread knotting on each thread in turn, until you have made two half-hitches on thread No.6 (blue).
10 Leave thread No.1 on the left. Push up all the knots. It is important to keep the tension even throughout.

11 Start again on the left with the yellow thread which has now become thread No 1.
12 Continue until you are near the end of the threads.
13 Gather the threads together and knot. Use the loop and the knot to attach the armband to the wrist.

You can use many more colours than we have but it takes time to become neat so it is a good idea to begin with less.

Papier Mâché

The term papier mâché is French and means 'chewed paper'. The method given below is for making jewellery, which is not what one normally associates with papier mâché. However with a little practice you can make spectacular jewellery for only a few pence.

YOU WILL NEED
thin card   old tissue boxes, cereal boxes, shoe boxes etc
tissues
wallpaper paste OR flour and water mixed to a thick cream paste with a few drops of cloves added to preserve it (drops of cloves are available from chemists)
newspaper cut or ripped roughly into 5mm width strips.
white poster or acrylic paint
poster colours, designers' gouache or felt-tip pens
paint brushes
clear varnish (nail varnish will do)
jewellery findings (brooch backs and earring backs)
brown tape or a stapler if making bracelets
strong glue for attaching the jewellery findings

TO MAKE
1   Mix the wallpaper paste or flour and water.
2   Draw very simple shapes for earrings and brooches onto card.
3   Shred a tissue and dip it into the paste. Stick pieces of tissue into the centre of the shape you have just made. Leave to dry. You can put small pieces to dry on a piece of paper on top of a radiator.
4   When the tissue paper is dry, wrap strips of newspaper dipped in the paste round your shape. Leave to dry.

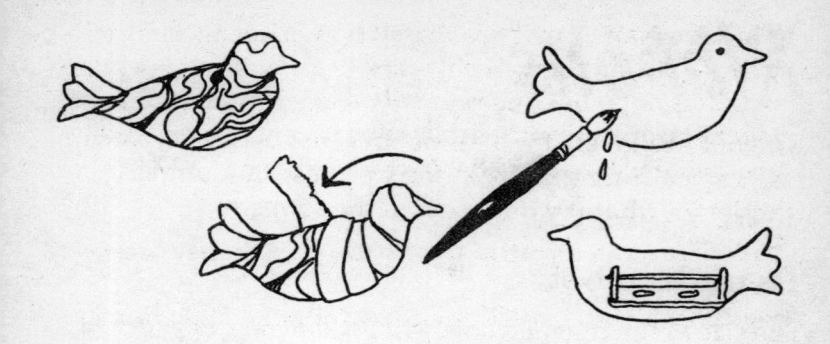

5 When the newspaper is dry, paint the top of your shape with white poster paint. Leave to dry, turn over and paint the other side white. Leave to dry.
6 Decorate with the poster paints or designers' gouache. Leave each colour to dry before painting the next one so that you don't get muddy results. Use simple shapes and patterns and lots of contrasting colours.
7 When the paint is dry, cover with varnish (clear nail varnish will do).
8 Stick your finding on the back of your shape. your brooch or earring is now complete.

TO MAKE A BRACELET

Bend the card round your wrist so that it fits, and will slip over your hand with room to spare. Staple or stick the ends together so you have formed a circle. Then follow steps 3 to 7 above.

Ribbons

Ribbons are lovely for making presents because you can make something that looks very professional for a fraction of what it would cost in the shops.

To make a bow

The size of the finished bow will depend on the width of the ribbon you use so choose narrow ribbon for a small bow and wide ribbon for a full bow.

YOU WILL NEED
1 piece of ribbon 12.5cm long
1 piece of ribbon 5cm long
thread for sewing

TO MAKE
1 Fold the larger piece of ribbon in half with the right sides together and sew the two ends with a running stitch as close to the edge as possible.
2 Fold the smaller piecce of ribbon in half with the right sides together and sew the two ends with a running stitch as close to the edge as possible.

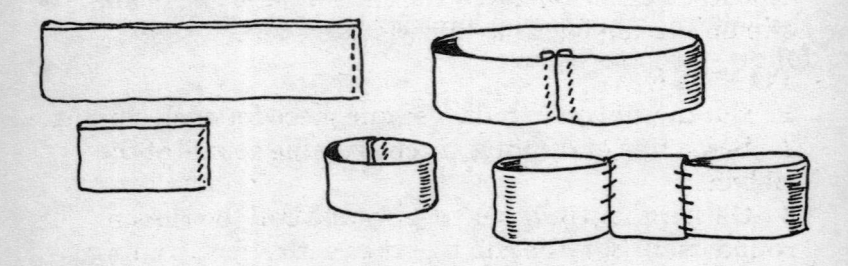

3 Turn both pieces of ribbon so they are the right way round with the seam lines in the centre.

4 Slip the 5cm piece of ribbon over the longer piece of ribbon so that both seams are at the back of the bow. Secure the small piece to the large piece with a few stitches.

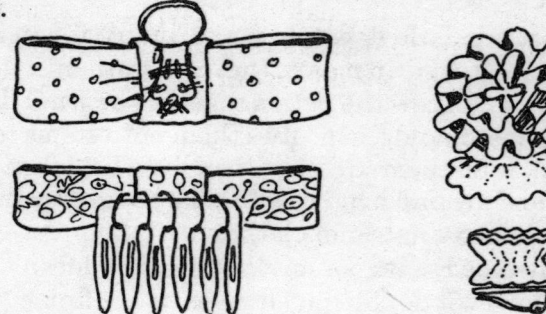

Ideas

✱ Sew bows onto plain hair combs.

✱ Make shoe bows by sewing the bent or perforated part of a clip-on earring base of the bow. The flat part will lie against your foot when you clip it on.

✱ Make a bow tie by sewing the bow onto elastic.

✱ Decorate an old cardigan with lots of brightly coloured bows.

Rosette ribbon earrings

YOU WILL NEED
100cm of 1.5cm ribbon **OR** 100 cm of 2cm satin ribbon.
clip-on earring backs with perforated cups.

TO MAKE
1 Cut the ribbon in half. Use one piece for each earring.
2 Sew a line of running stitches up the centre of the ribbon.
3 Gather the stitches up evenly and coil the ribbon round itself. Sew the coil together with a few running stitches.
4 Sew the ribbon coil onto the perforated cup. Attach the cup, by means of its clips, to the earring back.

RIBBON FLOWERS

***The Rose

The most versatile flower to make out of ribbon is the rose. Polyester satin makes the most authentic-looking roses. You can sew the petals together or wind florists wire round to hold them. Join them onto stems to make a bouquet, bind them together to make a bride's tiara, or wrap them around a hair comb. Sew them together to decorate shoes, hats and clothes.

Single-faced satin is easy to work as it doesn't slip too much, however double-faced gives a nice finish.

The size of the finished rose depends on the width of the ribbon used. Most roses are made from 12mm, 16mm and 38mm widths of ribbon. Each rose will take between 45cm-70cm depending on the size and fullness of bloom required.

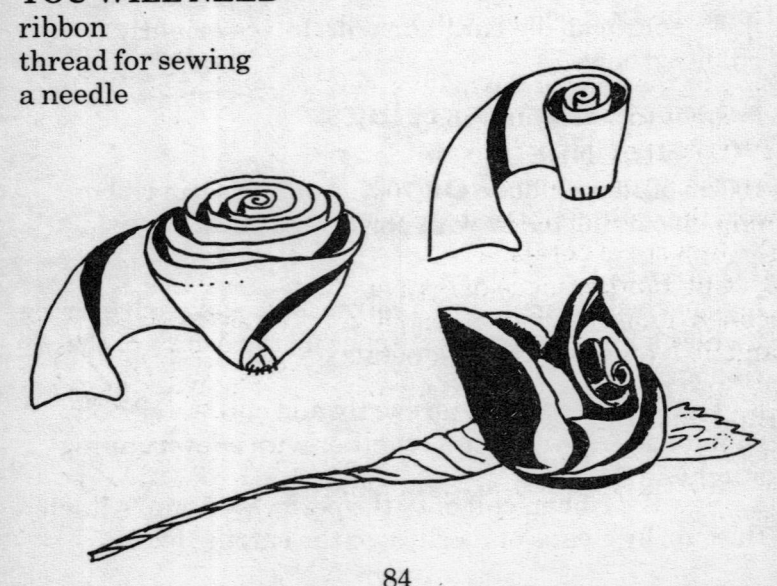

YOU WILL NEED
ribbon
thread for sewing
a needle

TO MAKE
1   Cut a piece of ribbon of any of the above widths 70cm long.
2   Roll one end of the ribbon six times and secure it at the base with a few stitches.
3   To form petals, fold the top edge of the unwound ribbon down and towards you so that the folded edge is at 45 degrees to the rolled tube.
4   Roll the tube across the fold, and roll and tack, shaping the rose as you work.
5   Turn the raw edge under to finish.

Ribbon violets

YOU WILL NEED
16mm mauve ribbon
1.5mm yellow ribbon

TO MAKE
1   Cut a 15cm length of mauve ribbon and a 15cm piece of yellow ribbon.
2   Cut the ends of the mauve ribbon into a diagonal shape.
3   Fold the ribbon into an S–shape and bind in the middle with the yellow ribbon to make the first set of petals.
3   Cut another piece of mauve ribbon, fold this in an S–shape and lie it on top of the first petals at right angles so it forms a cross. Bind this cross onto the first set of petals.
5   Sew the violets onto haircombs or grips.

Cheap And Cheerful!

FOOD

You can make jewellery from sweets, nuts, raisins, pasta, popcorn. You can give the jewellery a coat of clear varnish, nail varnish will do. or keep it as it is and eat it when hungry.

Edible sweet necklace

YOU WILL NEED
plastic or embroidery thread
mints or boiled sweets with holes through the centre

TO MAKE
Thread the sweets onto the thread and tie the ends together.

Pasta jewellery

Pasta comes in many different shapes and sizes. Use pasta bows to make brooches or hair slides. Use pasta with holes such as macaroni, wheels and stars for threading to make bracelets and necklaces.

Wheel bracelet

YOU WILL NEED
36 Pasta wheels
poster paint
paint brush

TO MAKE
1 Paint the pasta wheels around the edges and leave to dry.
2 Thread onto shirring elastic and tie ends together.

Pasta Bow Brooch

YOU WILL NEED
gold and pink poster paint, a brush, 1 pasta bow
PVA glue, a brooch back

TO MAKE
1 Paint the bow with pink poster paint and leave it to dry.
2 Paint dots on with the gold, poster paint, and leave to dry.
3 Paint with clear nail varnish.
4 Turn brooch over and stick on brooch back.

NATURAL SOURCES

Jewellery can be made from almost anything! Look at natural sources, such as shells, bits of driftwood, feathers, bamboo, pieces of bone, animal teeth, seeds or even small pebbles with holes. With the exception of the pebbles, all of these may be turned into beads by drilling with a hand drill using the finest drill bit you can find. Your local hardware shop will sell drill bits. Thread any of the beads onto raffia, leather thonging or shoelaces to create an ethnic look.

A leather earring

YOU WILL NEED
scraps of leather in toning colours.
pinking shears
leather punch
1 head pin
1 bead cup
round-nosed pliers
a kidney wire (for pierced ears) or a screw or clip (for unpierced ears)

TO MAKE
1   With the pinking shears, cut the leather into rough shapes approximately 1cm square. Do not worry if they are not all the same, the slightly eccentric shape is part of the design! Cut about 10 of these.
2   Turn the leather punch on to its smallest hole setting, and punch a hole through the middle of each piece of leather.

3 Thread the bead cup onto the head pin, so that it looks like a miniature saucer. Thread the first leather piece on top of this with its right side facing down. Thread the second and subsequent pieces of leather onto the pin with their right side facing up.
4 Bend the top of the head pin round the pliers so that it forms a loop.
5 Thread the loop on the kidney wire or earclip and close the loop.

TO MAKE A NECKLACE
Thread the leather scraps onto a leather thong or piece of nylon gut.

BALLOONS

This jewellery looks really great and costs very little to make. You can use old balloons left over from a party.

Balloon earrings

YOU WILL NEED
(The quantities given are for one earring.
Double the amounts for a pair of earrings.)
earring clips or wires
4 balloons (try to use clashing colours such as luminous pink and orange, or lime green and citrus yellow)
1 head pin
1 bead cup
2 or 3 small beads (again, clashing colours look good)

TO MAKE
1   With scissors or pinking shears, cut down the length of the balloons making strips of about 5mm wide.
2   Thread the head cup onto the head pin.
3   With a pin or a pair of scissors, make a small hole in the centre of each piece of balloon.
4   Thread about 20 pieces of balloon onto each head pin.
5   Add the beads to the head pin.

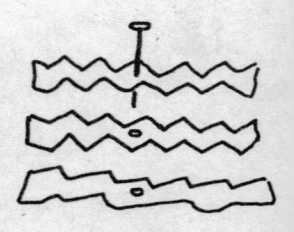

6 Either curl the remaining section of head pin round some round-nosed pliers and pull to get a spring like effect, or bend the remaining section of head pin into zigzag shapes.

7 Make a loop at the end of the head pin and thread onto the earring wire or clip.

**Balloon necklace

YOU WILL NEED
1 packet of balloons
1 eye pin
1 earring hook
1 piece of black 2 core lighting cable 40cm long, or larger if required

TO MAKE
1 Using a pair of dressmaker's scissors, cut the necks off the round balloons.
2 Then cut the necks into 5mm strips (so they look like miniature armbands).
3 Cut the long balloons in the same way – you can use all of the ballon except the round end.
4 Thread these pieces onto the cable. If they are loose, twist them into a double or treble loop before threading them, so that they fit.
5 Split one of the remaining balloon bodies so that you have two flat circles, but cutting along the fold line.

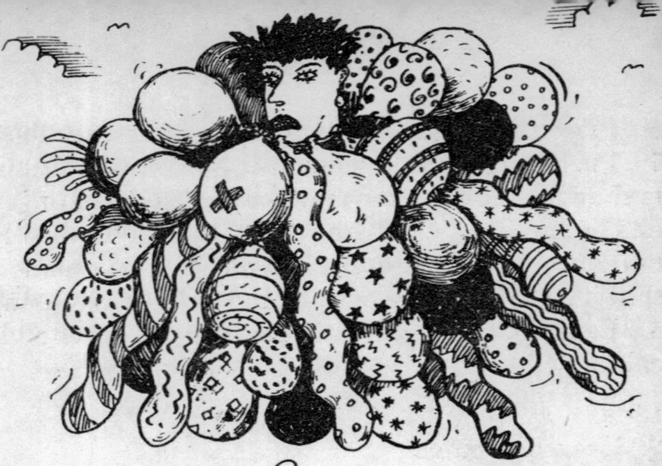

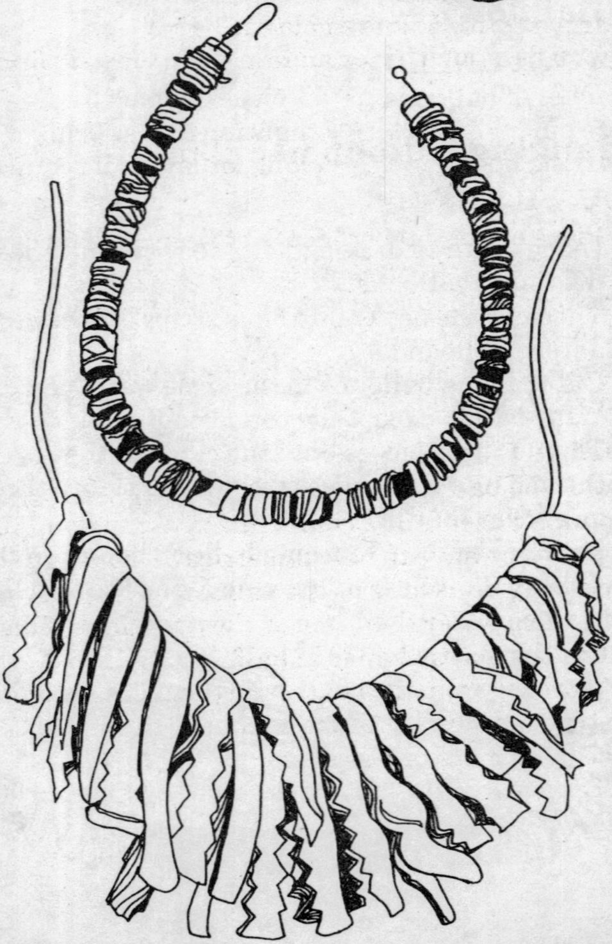

6 Pierce a hole in the centre of each circle with a pin.
7 Push the eye pin through the hole until only the loop is showing, holding the stalk of the eye pin alongside one end of the cable. Cover the end of the cable with the balloon circle. Roll up the last piece of balloon neck so that it holds both the eye pin and balloon circle in place.
8 Repeat 6 and 7, using the hook at the other end of the cable.

Ideas
* Use white cable
* thread with coloured elastic bands.
* Use flex (such as for an iron or an electric fire).

*Hanging balloon necklace

YOU WILL NEED
1 Piece of fine rubber lace 64cm long. (If you can't get rubber use plastic or leather thonging).
1 packet of balloons (if you made the necklace 1 use the left overs for this one).
1 packet of coloured elastic bands (optional)
1 pair of scissors.

TO MAKE
1 Cut the balloons into long thin strips, using scissors or pinking shears or a combination of the two. *Note*: The strips do not have to be symmetrical. The length of the pieces may be as long as the balloon or less. Try not to make them wider than 1cm or they will look clumsy.
2 Cut the elastic bands in half.
3 Working from the centre, tie the pieces of balloon and elastic bands onto the lace so that both ends of each piece hang more or less evenly.
4 To wear, tie the ends of the lace together around the neck.

**TIGHTS

Flowers made from tights and wire can be used on hats, hair slides or sewn onto alice bands or elastic to wear in your hair. Or you can sew them onto safety pins to make brooches.

YOU WILL NEED
millinery wire or any other (fine gauge) thin wire (fuse wire will do)
assorted beads (some rocailles, some ordinary)
scraps of coloured stockings or tights (the brighter the better)
floral tape (you can buy this by the reel from good florists)
wire cutters
scissors
ruler
bead pins

TO MAKE
1   For each flower cut 6 pieces of wire about 6cm long.
2   Fold each piece of wire in half, twist the two ends together and then open out to form a petal shape.
3   Cut a piece of fabric that is twice the size of the petal shape.
4   Fold the fabric over the shape and pull the loose edges down to the bottom of the stem.

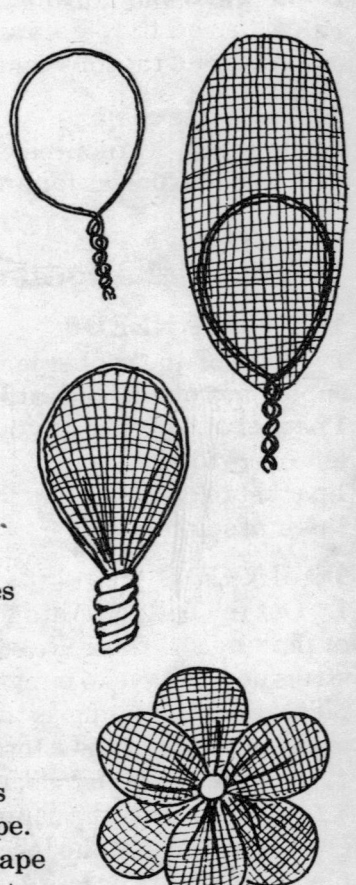

5 Wrap a piece of wire round the stem to secure the fabric in place.
6 Make all the other petals in the same way.
7 Thread a large and a small bead onto a head pin to make a stem.
8 Arrange the petals around the stem and then bind onto the stem with wire.
9 When all the petals are in place, wrap the florist's tape around the loose ends to neaten and finish off.

Suppliers

Beads are now sold in many craft shops and haberdashery departments of large stores. The following suppliers also provide a mail order service.

The Bead Shop
43 Neal Street
London WC2H 9PJ

Ells and Farrier Ltd
(Shop)
5 Princes Street,
Hanover Square,
London W1

(Mail order)
Unit 26
Chiltern Trading Estate
Earl Howe Road
Holmer Green
High Wycombe
Buckinghamshire

(Mail order and retail shop)
11 Blue Boar Street
Oxford
Tel: 0865-247 292

Janet Coles Beads
Perdiswell Cottage
Bilford Road
Worcester WE3 8QA
Tel: 0905 54024

Hobby Horse
(Retail and wholesale shop)
15-17 Langton Street
London SW10 0LJ
Tel: 01-351 6951